the really hungry
STUDENT COOKBOOK

the really hungry
STUDENT COOKBOOK

HOW TO EAT WELL ON A BUDGET

RYLAND PETERS & SMALL
LONDON • NEW YORK

Senior Designer Iona Hoyle
Editor Ellen Parnavelas
Head of Production Patricia Harrington
Art Director Leslie Harrington
Editorial Director Julia Charles

Indexer Hilary Bird

First published in 2013
by Ryland Peters & Small
20–21 Jockey's Fields
London WC1R 4BW
and
519 Broadway, 5th Floor
New York NY 10012

www.rylandpeters.com

Text © Amanda Grant, Annie Rigg, Dan May,
Sunil Vijayakar, Fiona Smith, Hannah Miles,
Miranda Ballard, Ghillie Basan, Susannah Blake,
Ross Dobson, Tonia George, Laura Washburn and
Ryland Peters & Small 2013

Design and photographs © Ryland Peters
& Small 2013

ISBN: 978-1-84975-440-8
10 9 8 7 6 5 4 3 2 1

A CIP record for this book is available from
the British Library.

US Library of Congress Cataloging-in-Publication data
has been applied for.

Printed and bound in China

NOTES:

■ All spoon measurements are level, unless otherwise specified.

■ Ovens should be preheated to the specified temperature. Recipes in this book were tested using a regular oven. If using a fan-assisted oven, follow the manufacturer's instructions for adjusting temperatures.

■ All eggs are medium UK/large US, unless otherwise specified. Recipes containing raw or partially cooked egg should not be served to the very young, very old, anyone with a compromised immune system or pregnant women.

■ Whenever a recipe calls for olive oil, if you are using it raw (e.g. in a salad dressing or drizzled over vegetables), the extra virgin variety is the tastiest. For frying or roasting, use a basic (not extra virgin), mild variety.

■ Where a recipe calls for salt and black pepper, use sea salt and freshly ground black pepper if at all possible. They give the best flavour.

contents

INTRODUCTION

If you're living away from home for the first time, you're going to want to know how to cook up a storm in the kitchen and this book is here to show you how. Whether you want to know how to make a stack of pancakes on a lazy Sunday morning, a warming casserole to fight off those homesick blues or some tasty snacks for your movie night, this book has all you need. It will banish any fears you might have if you're new to cooking, and if you're already getting A grades in culinary arts, you're sure to find some fresh inspiration here. All the recipes are exciting and delicious! Some are super-quick, while others need a little bit more time but are definitely worth the wait. Either way, this collection of stress-free recipes won't leave you hungry and will be cheaper and healthier than living on take-out. Check out all the hot tips in Kitchen Know-how on the following pages before you get started – they will make life a whole lot easier and ensure that you can always whip up something tasty, even with very few ingredients.

KITCHEN KNOW-HOW

The recipes in this book need the minimum of kitchen equipment. Some recipes, like the desserts, will require extras, e.g. a handheld electric whisk (which can be bought very cheaply), or a baking pan for brownies, etc. but you can go a long way with the following essential items:

CHECK LIST

KITCHEN KIT

★ 2 or 3 sharp knives, including a serrated knife
☑ wooden spoon
★ fish/egg slice
☑ potato masher
★ garlic crusher
☑ pepper mill
★ can opener
☑ vegetable peeler
★ cheese grater
☑ 2 chopping boards (1 for meat and 1 for veg)
★ large mixing bowl
☑ sieve/strainer
★ colander
☑ 1 large and 1 medium saucepan
★ frying pan/skillet with a lid
☑ baking sheet

★ roasting pan
☑ ovenproof dish (Pyrex or ceramic)
★ measuring jug/pitcher
☑ weighing scales
★ a selection of airtight containers
☑ kettle
★ toaster
☑ kitchen foil
★ clingfilm/plastic wrap
☑ greaseproof paper
★ kitchen paper/paper towels
☑ cleaning stuff, including washing up liquid, sponges and multi-surface cleaner
★ dish towels
☑ oven gloves

HANDY INGREDIENTS

★ sea salt
★ black peppercorns
★ olive oil
★ vegetable or sunflower oil
★ balsamic vinegar
★ red or white wine vinegar
★ dark or light soy sauce
★ tomato ketchup (as if you needed reminding!)
★ mustard
★ mayonnaise
★ long grain rice

★ risotto rice
★ dried pasta, including spaghetti
★ couscous
★ stock cubes or bouillon powder
★ canned chopped tomatoes
★ a selection of canned beans, such as cannellini, pinto and kidney
★ canned tuna
★ plain/all-purpose flour
★ self raising/rising flour
★ sugar

★ tomato purée/paste
★ a selection of dried herbs, such as oregano
★ a selection of dried spices, such as curry powder, ground cumin, paprika, chilli/chili powder or dried chilli/hot pepper flakes
★ Marmite
★ honey
★ butter or margarine
★ milk
★ onions
★ garlic

8

FOOD SAFETY

■ **Always keep your kitchen clean!** Keep it tidy and disinfect work surfaces after use with a mild detergent or an antibacterial cleaner. Keep pets off surfaces and, as far as possible, keep them out of the kitchen.

■ Store food safely to avoid cross-contamination. Keep food in clean, dry, airtight containers, always store raw and cooked foods separately and wash utensils (and your hands) between preparing raw and cooked foods. Never put cooked food on a surface that you have used to prepare raw meat, fish or poultry without thoroughly washing and drying the surface first.

■ Wash your hands with hot, soapy water before and after handling food, and after you have handled raw meat and fish.

■ Never put hot food into a fridge, as this will increase the internal temperature to an unsafe level. Cool leftover food quickly to room temperature, ideally by transferring it to a cold dish, then refrigerate. Cool large dishes such as stews by putting the dish in a sink of cold water. Stir occasionally (change the water often to keep the temperature low), then refrigerate once cool. During cooling, cover the food loosely with clingfilm/plastic wrap to protect it.

■ Don't use perishable food beyond the 'use-by' date as it could be a health risk. If you have any doubts about the food, discard it.

■ Reheated food must be piping hot throughout before consumption. Never reheat any type of food more than once.

■ Frozen meat and poultry should be defrosted before you cook them otherwise the centre may not be cooked, which could be dangerous.

■ If you are going to freeze food, freeze food that is in prime condition, on the day of purchase, or as soon as a dish is made and cooled. Freeze it quickly and in small quantities, if possible. Label and date food and keep plenty of supplies in the freezer.

■ Always leave a gap in the container when freezing liquids, so that there is enough room for the liquid to expand as it freezes.

■ Always let food cool before freezing it. Warm or hot food will increase the internal temperature of the freezer and may cause other foods to begin to defrost and spoil.

■ Use proper oven gloves to remove hot dishes from the oven – don't just use a dish towel because you risk burning yourself. Dish towels are also a breeding ground for germs so only use them for drying, and wash them often.

■ Hard cheeses such as Cheddar, Gruyère and Parmesan will keep for up to 3 weeks if stored correctly. Once opened, fresh, soft cheeses such as cream cheese should be consumed within 3 days.

■ Leftover canned foods should be transferred to an airtight container, kept in the fridge and eaten within 2 days. Once cans are opened, the contents should be treated as fresh food. This doesn't apply to food sold in tubs with resealable lids, such as cocoa powder.

■ The natural oils in chillies/chiles may cause irritation to your skin and eyes. When preparing them, wear disposable gloves or pull a small plastic bag over each hand, secured with an elastic band around the wrist, to create a glove.

If your kitchen is prone to over-heating, it is best to store eggs in their box in the fridge. Keep them pointed-end downwards and away from strong-smelling foods, as they can absorb odours. Always use by the 'best-before' date.

Wash hands before and after handling eggs, and discard any cracked and/or dirty eggs.

Cooked rice is a potential source of food poisoning. Cool leftovers quickly (ideally within an hour), then store in an airtight container in the fridge and use within 24 hours. Always reheat cooked cold rice until piping hot.

INGREDIENTS TIPS

When substituting dried herbs for fresh, use roughly half the quantity the recipe calls for, as dried herbs have a more concentrated flavour.

Chop leftover fresh herbs, spoon them into an ice-cube tray, top each portion with a little water and freeze. Once solid, put the cubes in a freezer bag. Seal, label and return to the freezer. Add the frozen herb cubes to soups, casseroles and sauces.

The colour of a fresh chilli/chile is no indication of how hot it will be. Generally speaking, the smaller and thinner the chilli/chile, the hotter it will be.

To reduce the heat of a fresh chilli, cut it in half lengthways, then scrape out and discard the seeds and membranes (or core). See also 'food safety' above for advice on handling chillies/chiles.

Most vegetables keep best in the fridge, but a cool, dark place is also good if you lack fridge space. Potatoes should always be stored in the dark, otherwise they go green or sprout, making them inedible.

To skin tomatoes, score a cross in the base of each one using a sharp knife. Put them in a heatproof bowl, cover with boiling water, leave for about 30 seconds, then transfer them to a bowl of cold water. When cool enough to handle, drain and peel off the skins with a knife.

To clean leeks, trim them, then slit them lengthways about a third of the way through. Open the leaves a little and wash away any dirt from between the layers under cold running water.

Store flour in its original sealed packaging or in an airtight container in a cool, dry, airy place. Ideally, buy and store small quantities at a time, to help avoid infestation of psocids (very small, barely visible, grey-brown insects), which may appear even in the cleanest of homes. If you do find these small insects in your flour, dispose of it immediately and wash and dry the container thoroughly. Never mix new flour with old.

If you run out of self-raising/self-rising flour, sift together 2 teaspoons of baking powder with every 225 g/scant 2 cups plain/all-purpose flour. This will not be quite as effective but it is a good substitute.

Store raw meat and fish on the bottom shelf in the fridge to prevent it dripping onto anything below.

Store coffee (beans and ground) in the fridge or freezer, or it will go stale very quickly.

Store oils, well sealed, in a cool, dark, dry place, away from direct sunlight. They can be kept in the fridge (though this is not necessary), but oils such as olive oil tend to solidify and go cloudy in the fridge. If this happens, bring the oil back to room temperature before use.

To de-vein large prawns/shrimp, cut along the back of each shell using a sharp knife and lift or scrape out the dark vein. Alternatively, use a skewer to pierce the flesh at the head of the prawn/shrimp, just below the vein, then use the skewer to gently remove the vein.

Small pasta tubes and twists such as penne and fusilli are good for chunky vegetable sauces and some meat- and cream-based sauces. Larger tubes such as rigatoni are ideal for meat sauces. Smooth, creamy, butter- or olive oil-based sauces and meat sauces are ideal for long strands such as spaghetti (so the sauce can cling to the pasta).

Dried pasta has a long shelf life and should be stored in its unopened packet or in an airtight container in a cool, dry place. Leftover cooked pasta should be kept in a sealed container in the fridge and used within 2 days. Ordinary cooked pasta does not freeze well on its own, but it freezes successfully in dishes such as lasagne and cannelloni. Allow 85–115 g/3–4 oz. of dried pasta per person.

Pasta must be cooked in a large volume of salted, boiling water. Keep the water at a rolling boil throughout cooking. Once you have added the pasta to the boiling water, give it a stir, then cover the pan to help the water return to the boil as quickly as possible. Remove the lid once the water has started boiling again (to prevent the water boiling over), and stir occasionally. Check the manufacturer's instructions for cooking times. When it is ready, cooked pasta should be al dente – tender but with a slight resistance.

As an accompaniment, allow 55–85 g/¼–⅓ cup uncooked rice per person or for a main like risotto, up to 115 g/½ cup.

Rice may be rinsed before cooking to remove tiny pieces of grit or excess starch. Most packaged rice is checked and clean, however, so rinsing it is unnecessary and will wash away nutrients. Risotto rice is not washed before use, but basmati rice usually is – rinse it under cold water until the water runs clear.

TASTE TIPS

Try mixing a pinch or two of ground spices such as curry powder, chilli/chili powder or turmeric with breadcrumbs or flour, and use to coat foods before frying. Add ground spices such as cinnamon, mixed spice or ginger to fruit crumble toppings. A pinch of ground nutmeg will perk up mashed potatoes, cheese sauce, cooked spinach and rice puddings.

Stir wholegrain mustard into mashed potatoes or mayonnaise before serving to add extra flavour. Mustard also enhances salad dressings and sauces. A pinch of mustard powder added to cheese dishes will enhance the flavour.

If you add too much salt to a soup or casserole, add one or two peeled and cubed potatoes to soak up the salt, cooking until tender. Discard the potatoes before serving.

An excellent way of thickening soups is to stir in a little oatmeal. It adds flavour too. A small amount of instant mashed potatoes stirred in at the last minute is also a good way of thickening soup.

Add a little barley to soups and stews – it will add flavour and texture and have a thickening effect.

A teaspoon or two of pesto stirred into each portion of a hot vegetable soup just before serving will liven it up.

For a tasty and creamy salad dressing, mash some blue cheese and stir it into mayonnaise, or a mixture of mayonnaise and plain yogurt.

Add some health and a satisfying crunch to salads by tossing in a handful or two of lightly toasted seeds or chopped nuts just before serving. Good ideas include sunflower, sesame or pumpkin seeds and hazelnuts, walnuts, pecan nuts or pistachios. Toasted seeds can also be sprinkled over cooked vegetables to add crunch to a dish.

If you over-cook an omelette, leave it to cool and use it as a sandwich filling. Chop the omelette and combine it with mayonnaise and snipped chives, if you like.

Bulk out a pasta or rice salad by adding a can of drained and rinsed beans such as chickpeas, red kidney beans or black-eye beans.

For an extra-crunchy crumble topping, replace 30 g/2 tablespoons of the flour with the same weight of chopped nuts, oats or oatmeal, or replace granulated sugar with light brown soft sugar.

KITCHEN WISDOM

◆ To remove odours from a container that you want to use again, fill the container with hot water, then stir in 1 tablespoon baking powder. Leave it to stand overnight, then wash, rinse well and dry before use.

◆ If you transfer foods from packages to storage containers, tape the food label onto the container so you can easily identify its contents and you have a record of the manufacturer's cooking instructions, if necessary. Make a note of the 'best-before' or 'use-by' date on the container, too.

◆ Choose stackable containers to maximize storage space. Remember that square or rectangular containers make better use of shelf space than round or oval containers.

◆ For convenient single servings, freeze portions of home-made soup in large, thick paper cups or small individual containers. Remove them from the freezer as required, defrost and reheat the soup thoroughly before serving.

◆ To make salad dressings or vinaigrettes, put all the ingredients in a clean screw-top jar, seal and shake well. Alternatively, put the ingredients straight into the salad bowl and whisk together well, before adding the salad.

◆ Spirits with an alcohol content of 35% or over can be kept in the freezer – this is ideal for those which should be served ice-cold.

◆ To remove fishy odours after preparing fish, rub the cut surface of a lemon over your hands, the knife and chopping board. Rubbing your hands with vinegar or salt, then rinsing and washing them, will also help to get rid of unpleasant fishy smells.

◆ If you are short of space in the kitchen, cover the sink with a piece of wood cut to size or a large chopping board to create an extra work surface when the sink is not in use.

MICROWAVE SAFETY

◆ The more food you are cooking, and the colder it is, the longer it will take to cook in a microwave.

◆ When microwaving items such as sausages or bacon that may spit during cooking, cover them loosely with kitchen paper/paper towels, to avoid too much splattering.

◆ Many foods need to be covered during microwaving. Use microwave-safe clingfilm/plastic wrap, a plate or a lid. Pierce clingfilm/plastic wrap, or leave a gap at one side if using a plate or lid, to allow excess steam to escape.

◆ Never operate a microwave when it is empty, as the microwaves will bounce back to and damage the oven components.

◆ Be careful when stirring heated liquids in a container in the microwave, as they can bubble up without warning.

◆ After food has been removed from the microwave, it will continue to cook due to the residual heat within the food, so adhere to standing times when they are given in recipes.

◆ Use a microwave with a built-in turntable if possible, and make sure that you turn or stir the food several times during cooking to ensure even cooking throughout. The food towards the outer edges usually cooks first.

◆ Metal containers, china with a metallic trim, foil or crystal glass (which contains lead) should not be used in a microwave. Metal reflects microwaves and may damage the oven components. Microwave-safe plastic containers, ovenproof glass and ceramic dishes are all suitable, as is most household glazed china. Paper plates and kitchen paper/paper towels can be used to reheat food for short periods.

There is nothing quite as satisfying as sharing a hearty stack of pancakes with friends on a lazy Sunday morning.

blueberry PANCAKES

125 g/1 cup self-raising/self-rising flour

1 teaspoon baking powder

2 tablespoons sugar

¼ teaspoon sea salt

1 egg

100 ml/scant ½ cup milk

45 g/3 tablespoons butter, melted

150 g/1 generous cup blueberries, plus extra, to serve

maple syrup or honey, to serve

Preheat the oven to 110°C (225°F) Gas ¼.

Sift the flour and baking powder into a large mixing bowl and stir in the sugar and salt. Put the egg, milk and 75 ml/⅓ cup water in another bowl and beat to combine.

Stir half the butter into the wet ingredients in the bowl. Mix the wet ingredients with the dry ingredients until no lumps of flour remain.

Wipe a heavy-based frying pan/skillet with scrunched-up kitchen paper/paper towel dipped in the remaining melted butter. Heat up, then drop in 4 tablespoons of the batter in separate dollops. Cook for 1–2 minutes on the first side, then scatter over a few of the blueberries and flip the pancake over. Cook for 2 minutes, until golden and cooked through. Keep warm in the oven while you make the rest.

Serve with more blueberries and maple syrup or honey.

SERVES 1

BADASS BREAKFASTS

Porridge is healthy, cheap to make and it fills you up so it makes a winning breakfast all round. Top with sliced bananas or any other fresh or dried fruit of your choice.

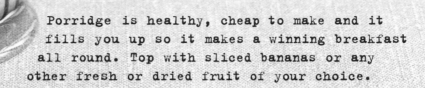

honey & banana
PORRIDGE

175 g/1 cup porridge oats/oatmeal

250 ml/1 cup milk

1 small ripe banana, mashed

a good pinch of ground cinnamon (optional)

To serve

honey or soft dark brown sugar

chilled milk (optional)

sliced banana, or other fresh or dried fruit

For the stovetop method, put the oats and milk in a saucepan and bring to the boil. Lower the heat and simmer, stirring often, for 2–3 minutes. Add the mashed banana and simmer for 1–2 minutes more, stirring often.

For the microwave method, combine the oats and milk in a glass bowl and microwave on high for 1½ minutes. Remove, stir in the banana and microwave for 1 minute.

Transfer to a serving bowl, sprinkle with the cinnamon if using, and top with a spoonful or so of honey or sugar. Serve immediately, with extra milk, if liked, and sliced bananas or any other fresh or dried fruit.

SERVES 4

Mmmm, crunchy honeyed granola. This recipe is sweet, rich and full of goodness so you don't need a lot to set you up for the day. The trick is to get it to brown evenly, so make sure you spread it out and turn it during roasting. Don't let it become too dark or it gets bitter. If in doubt, take it out and let it cool a little, then taste it and put it back in the oven.

nutty honey
GRANOLA

125 g/½ cup maple syrup

125 g/½ cup honey

4 tablespoons sunflower oil

250 g/2 cups rolled oats

75 g/⅔ cup shelled almonds, roughly chopped

75 g/⅔ cup shelled Brazil nuts, roughly chopped

50 g/⅓ cup pumpkin seeds

½ teaspoon sea salt

100 g/⅔ cup raisins

milk or yogurt, to serve

Preheat the oven to 140°C (275°F) Gas 1.

Put the maple syrup, honey and oil in a small saucepan and set over low heat to warm through. Put the oats, nuts, seeds and salt in a large mixing bowl and stir well. Pour over the warmed syrup and mix thoroughly with a wooden spoon. All the oats must be covered.

Spread the granola over 1–2 large baking sheets, lined with parchment paper, making sure it is no deeper than 1 cm/½ inch, and bake in the preheated oven for 20 minutes.

Remove the sheets from the oven and stir the toasted, golden granola from the edges to the middle, then smooth out again. Return to the oven for a further 15–20 minutes, until lightly golden. Don't expect it to become crunchy – the mixture will remain soft until it cools.

Remove from the oven and let cool for 10 minutes before stirring in the raisins. Let cool completely, then break into pieces. Serve with milk or yogurt and store the rest in an airtight container and eat within 1 month.

SERVES 10–12

Bring the fiesta to your breakfast table with this tasty Mexican-style dish. It's even better served with guacamole or sour cream.

HUEVOS RANCHEROS

3 tablespoons vegetable oil

1 green chilli/chile or jalapeño pepper, chopped

2 garlic cloves, crushed

500 g/1 lb. tomatoes, cut into wedges

1 x 400-g/14-oz. can pinto or cannellini beans

50 g/½ cup grated mature/sharp Cheddar

freshly squeezed juice of 1 lime, plus extra lime wedges to serve

a handful of fresh coriander/cilantro leaves, chopped

4 eggs

4 corn tortillas

sea salt and black pepper

Heat 1 tablespoon of the oil in a large frying pan/skillet over medium heat, then add the chilli/chile, half the garlic and a pinch of salt and fry for 1–2 minutes, until softened. Add the tomatoes and cook gently for about 20 minutes.

Heat the remaining oil in a small saucepan, add the remaining garlic and heat through for 20 seconds, until just browning. Add the beans, then using a potato masher, coarsely mash the beans and stir in plenty of salt and pepper and the Cheddar.

Stir the lime juice and coriander/cilantro into the tomato sauce. Make 4 holes in the sauce and crack an egg into each one. Cook for 3 minutes until set. Cover with the lid for the last 30 seconds just to firm up the whites.

Meanwhile, heat a frying pan/skillet over medium heat. Cook the tortillas for 1 minute on each side, until golden and hot. Transfer to 4 plates and spread the beans over the tortillas. Top with tomato salsa and the eggs. Serve with lime wedges and guacamole or sour cream, if liked.

SERVES 4

Scrambled eggs are a great, simple recipe to learn and can just as easily be served for lunch as for breakfast. Easy and delicious, these will keep you going through those long morning lectures.

herby SCRAMBLED EGGS

2 eggs

1 tablespoon freshly chopped flat-leaf parsley

4 cherry tomatoes, quartered

15 g/1 tablespoon butter

buttered toast, to serve

Break the eggs into a bowl. Add the parsley and beat lightly with a fork. Add the tomatoes and stir to mix.

Melt the butter in a saucepan over medium heat. Add the eggs and cook, stirring with a spoon. Keep stirring to break up the eggs.

When the eggs are almost cooked – so they look only slightly wet – take the pan off the heat and rest it on a pan stand. Keep stirring until the eggs are cooked – the heat from the pan will continue to cook them. Serve with plenty of hot, buttered toast.

SERVES 1

A hearty pork burger with all the traditional breakfast trimmings – for the days when cereal just won't cut it.

BIG BREAKFAST BURGER
with a portobello mushroom & a fried egg

2 tablespoons olive oil

5 mushrooms, finely chopped

200 g/7 oz. lean minced/ground pork

2 teaspoons tomato ketchup

a pinch of mustard powder

3 tablespoons fresh breadcrumbs

sea salt and black pepper

To serve

2 English muffins

tomato ketchup

2 fried eggs

2 grilled/broiled Portobello mushrooms

SERVES 2

Heat 1 tablespoon of the oil in a frying pan/skillet over medium heat. Add the chopped mushrooms and fry until soft and brown. Remove from the heat and set aside.

Put the pork in a bowl with the tomato ketchup, mustard powder, breadcrumbs and salt and pepper. Work together with your hands until evenly mixed. Add the cooled mushrooms and mix again. Divide the mixture in half and shape into two burger patties. Press each burger down to make them nice and flat.

Heat the remaining oil in the same frying pan/skillet and fry the burgers over medium–high heat for 5 minutes on each side until cooked through.

Slice the English muffins in half and lightly toast them under the grill/broiler or in the toaster. Spread a spoonful of tomato ketchup on the base of each muffin and put the cooked burgers on top. Put a fried egg and a grilled/broiled Portobello mushroom on top of each burger and finish with the lids of the English muffins. Serve with extra tomato ketchup on the side.

Stuffed tomatoes are an old-fashioned idea, but so simple and delicious. The secret is to slightly undercook them so that they don't collapse. If goat cheese is too expensive, you can use crumbled feta or cream cheese instead.

BAKED TOMATOES
stuffed with goat cheese & herbs

6 large tomatoes

2 tablespoons olive oil, plus extra for drizzling

1 onion, finely chopped

1 tablespoon freshly chopped thyme leaves

200 g/7 oz. goat cheese

4 tablespoons dried breadcrumbs

2 eggs, beaten

a handful of fresh basil leaves

Preheat the oven to 180°C (350°F) Gas 4.

Slice the top third off the tomatoes and set aside to use later. Scoop out the seeds and juices and discard or save for making a tomato sauce another time.

Heat the oil in a frying pan/skillet, add the onion and thyme and cook over medium heat for 5 minutes until softened. Remove from the heat and let cool slightly.

In a mixing bowl, beat the goat cheese, breadcrumbs and eggs together and season well. Stir in the onion mixture and a few of the basil leaves. Divide the stuffing between the hollow tomatoes and top with the reserved tomato lids. Arrange in a baking dish, drizzle with oil and scatter over the remaining basil leaves. Bake in the preheated oven for 18–20 minutes and serve immediately.

SERVES 4–6

WINNING LUNCHES

Another dish that makes an easy and delicious lunch, these juicy, fragrant mushrooms are really rich and garlicky. Pile them up on thick slices of hot buttered wholemeal/wholewheat toast or crusty bread — and if you're feeling really indulgent, add a spoonful of sour cream as well.

MUSHROOMS
on toast

1 tablespoon olive oil

2 shallots, finely sliced

1 garlic clove, finely chopped

150 g/1 cup button mushrooms

60 ml/¼ cup white wine

1 teaspoon freshly chopped thyme leaves, plus extra to serve (optional)

2 thick slices of wholemeal/ wholewheat bread

butter, for spreading

sour cream, to serve (optional)

sea salt and black pepper

Heat the oil in a frying pan/skillet, add the shallots and fry gently for 2 minutes, then add the garlic and cook for a further minute.

Add the mushrooms, toss to coat in the garlicky oil, then add the white wine, thyme and a pinch of salt. Increase the heat and bring to the boil, then simmer gently for about 10 minutes until the mushrooms are tender and the juices have been absorbed.

When the mushrooms are nearly cooked, toast the bread on both sides and spread with the butter. Season the mushrooms with pepper, check if they need any more salt, then pile onto the toast. Top with fresh thyme, if using, and serve immediately with sour cream, if liked.

SERVES 2

The wonderful baked potato nearly always saves the day, especially when you're hungry. For an extra-hearty meal, add a can of tuna to the potatoes when you mix in the other ingredients.

Cajun-spiced
BAKED POTATOES

2 large baking potatoes, scrubbed

15 g/1 tablespoon butter

1 big teaspoon Dijon mustard

2 teaspoons Cajun spice blend

2 spring onions/scallions, chopped

1 fresh green chilli/chile, deseeded and chopped

100 g/1 cup grated mature/sharp Cheddar, plus extra for sprinkling

1 egg, lightly beaten

sea salt and black pepper

SERVES 2

Preheat the oven to 200°C (400°F) Gas 6.

Pierce the potato skins several times with a fork, then put the potatoes directly on a shelf in the preheated oven. Bake for about 50–70 minutes, until the flesh is soft enough to scrape out and the skins are crispy enough to retain their shape. Leave the oven on.

Once the potatoes are soft, let cool slightly until they are cool enough to handle. Cut in half lengthways and spoon the insides into a large bowl. Mash the potato until it is fairly lump-free, then add the butter, mustard, Cajun spice blend, spring onions/scallions, chilli/chile and Cheddar. Stir together until well mixed. Mix the beaten egg through the mashed potato mixture and then spoon the mixture back into the skins.

Sprinkle some extra grated Cheddar over the filled potatoes and top with the reserved chilli/chile pieces, if using. Put the potatoes on a baking sheet and return to the oven for a further 15–20 minutes or until the cheese starts to brown and serve hot.

These oozy, cheesy toasts make a simple tomato soup more filling and much more exciting! Serve them floating on the top of the soup or on the side for dunking.

PIZZA SOUP

2–3 tablespoons olive or vegetable oil

500 g/1 lb. onions, thinly sliced

a handful of freshly chopped flat-leaf parsley leaves (optional)

a splash of red wine (optional)

1 x 400-g/14-oz. can chopped tomatoes

1 tablespoon tomato ketchup

a pinch of sugar

1 litre/4 cups vegetable stock

1 baguette, sliced into rounds, allow 1–2 slices per serving

125-g/4½-oz. ball mozzarella, sliced

a pinch of dried oregano

pitted and sliced black olives, to serve (optional)

sea salt and black pepper

SERVES 6–8

Heat the oil in a large saucepan and add the onions. Cook over low heat until soft. Stir in the parsley and wine, if using, and season lightly with salt and pepper. Cook until the liquid has evaporated. Stir in the tomatoes, ketchup, sugar and stock. Bring to the boil, then reduce the heat and simmer for at least 20 minutes until thick. Taste and adjust the seasoning.

Just before serving, preheat the grill/broiler to medium–hot. Top each slice of bread with mozzarella, sprinkle lightly with oregano and a few olive slices, if using. Ladle the soup into heatproof serving bowls. Float the cheese-topped bread slices on top of the soup and put the bowls under the grill/broiler until the cheese is browned and bubbling. Serve immediately, taking care as the bowls will be hot.

Alternatively, put the cheese-topped bread slices under the grill/broiler until browned and bubbling and serve alongside the soup for dunking.

Chorizo is a spicy sausage, often smoked or cured and flavoured with paprika. It gives a lovely, smoky flavour to this rich and warming soup, which is perfect served with chunks of crusty bread.

chickpea, tomato & chorizo
SOUP

200 g/7 oz. chorizo, roughly chopped

1 onion, chopped

2 garlic cloves, peeled and crushed

1 x 400-g/14-oz. can chopped tomatoes

2 sprigs fresh thyme

1 x 400-g/14-oz. can chickpeas, drained and rinsed

1 litre/4 cups vegetable stock

chunks of crusty bread, to serve (optional)

sea salt and black pepper

Put the chorizo in a large saucepan or casserole dish over medium heat and cook until it starts to release its oil. Continue to cook, stirring, for 4–5 minutes until crisp.

Add the onion and garlic and cook for 5–10 minutes over low heat until softened. Add the tomatoes and thyme and turn the heat back up to medium. Cook for 5 minutes to intensify the flavour, then add the chickpeas and stock. Return to the boil, cover and simmer for 15 minutes.

Remove the thyme. Season well with salt and pepper and simmer for a further 10 minutes. Ladle the soup into serving bowls and serve immediately with chunks of crusty bread, if liked.

SERVES 4

Couscous is a dish made from tiny grains of durum wheat that is cooked by steaming. It is healthy and filling and very quick to prepare — great for making salads a bit more substantial.

COUSCOUS SALAD
with feta, peas & spring beans

270 g/1½ cups couscous

400 ml/1¾ cups boiling water

75 ml/5 tablespoons olive oil

1 garlic clove, crushed

3 spring onions/scallions, thinly sliced

2 tablespoons freshly chopped dill

2 tablespoons freshly chopped chives

1 tablespoon freshly grated lemon zest

1 tablespoon freshly chopped lemon flesh

250 g/2 cups chopped feta

150 g/1 cup sugar snap peas

150 g/1 cup frozen broad/fava beans, defrosted

150 g/1 cup frozen peas, defrosted

black pepper

Put the couscous in a large bowl and pour over the boiling water. Cover with clingfilm/plastic wrap or a plate and leave to swell for 10 minutes.

Pour the olive oil into a mixing bowl and add the garlic, shallots, dill, chives and lemon and season with black pepper. Add the feta, turn in the oil and set aside while you cook the beans.

Bring a medium saucepan of unsalted water to the boil. Add the sugar snap peas, bring back to the boil and cook for 1 minute. Add the broad/fava beans, bring back to the boil and cook for 1 minute. Finally, add the peas and cook for 2 minutes. Drain.

Uncover the couscous and stir in the hot beans and peas. Transfer to serving bowls and top with the feta, spooning over the flavoured oil as you go. Stir well before serving.

SERVES 4

Rajas simply means strips of pepper.
Roast chicken works best in this
recipe but if time is an issue, you can
sauté the chicken on the stovetop instead.

CHIPOTLE CHICKEN
& rajas tacos

500 g/1 lb. 2 oz. boneless, skinless chicken, thinly sliced

2 teaspoons ground cumin

1 teaspoon chilli/chili powder

2 teaspoons sea salt

2 tablespoons vegetable oil

6–8 corn or flour tortillas, warmed

Rajas

1 red (bell) pepper, thinly sliced

1 yellow (bell) pepper, thinly sliced

2 tablespoons vegetable oil

2 garlic cloves, crushed

1 teaspoon dried oregano

To serve

sour cream

black pepper

hot sauce (such as Tabasco)

SERVES 4

Preheat the oven to 180°C (350°F) Gas 4.

To prepare the rajas, put the peppers in a large roasting pan. Add the oil, garlic, oregano and salt and toss well. Spread evenly in the pan and roast in the preheated oven for 20–30 minutes until the peppers begin to char. Remove from the oven and set aside until needed. Do not turn off the oven.

Put the chicken in a roasting pan. Add the cumin, chilli/chili powder, salt and oil and toss well. Spread in an even layer and roast for 15–20 minutes until browned and cooked through.

To serve, put a generous helping of sliced chicken in the middle of each tortilla. Top with rajas, a spoonful of sour cream and some black pepper. Serve immediately with extra sour cream and any hot sauce on the side.

VIVA LA FIESTA

Grilling the courgettes/zucchini and corn cobs gives them a smoky, chargrilled taste, which can be achieved using either a stovetop grill pan/griddle or a barbecue.

mixed vegetable
TACOS

1 kg/2 lb. 4 oz. courgettes/zucchini, halved and sliced

vegetable oil

2 corn cobs

sea salt

½ teaspoon ground cumin

10–12 small corn or flour tortillas, warmed

To serve

sour cream

ready-made tomato salsa

½ teaspoon chilli/chili powder

black pepper

Put the courgettes/zucchini in a mixing bowl and drizzle with oil. Mix well so they are lightly coated. Heat a stovetop grill pan/griddle until hot. Cook the courgette/zucchini slices for 3–5 minutes on each side until charred. Rub the corn cobs with oil, then cook for 10–15 minutes, turning often, until charred all over. Set aside.

Dice the charred courgette/zucchini slices and put them in a shallow dish. Scrape the charred kernels from the corn cobs and add to the courgettes/zucchini. Add the cumin. Season with salt and mix well.

To serve, put a generous helping of the vegetable mixture in the middle of each tortilla. Top with a spoonful of sour cream and tomato salsa, sprinkle with chilli/chili powder and black pepper and serve immediately.

SERVES 4

These tasty chicken tacos can be thrown together in no time and make the perfect meal to share with friends. For an easier option, feel free to use ready-cooked chicken instead.

shredded CHICKEN TACOS

600 g/1 lb. 5 oz. boneless, skinless chicken

chicken or vegetable stock, or water, as required

10–12 flour tortillas, warmed

200 g/2 cups crumbled feta

sea salt and black pepper

To serve

ready-made tomato salsa

ready-made guacamole

sprigs of fresh coriander/cilantro

hot sauce (such as Tabasco)

halved limes

Put the chicken in a saucepan and add enough stock or water to cover. If using water or unseasoned stock, season with salt.

Bring to the boil over medium heat, then cover and simmer gently for 30–40 minutes until cooked through and tender. Remove the chicken from the pan and let cool slightly, then shred using your hands or two forks. Taste and adjust the seasoning.

To serve, put a generous helping of the shredded chicken in the centre of each tortilla and sprinkle over a handful of crumbled cheese. Top with spoonfuls of tomato salsa and guacamole and a sprig of fresh coriander/cilantro. Serve immediately with extra tomato salsa and guacamole, any hot sauce and halved limes for squeezing.

SERVES 3–4

These hearty quesadillas are a great brunch or lunch dish. For a more authentic Mexican flavour, replace the baked beans with refried beans.

ham & egg brunch
QUESADILLAS

4 thick slices ham

8 large flour tortillas

200 g/2 cups grated Cheddar or Monterey Jack

1 x 400-g/14-oz. can baked beans in tomato sauce

1 tablespoon vegetable oil

50 g/4 tablespoons butter

4 eggs

Preheat the oven to 120°C (250°F) Gas ½.

To assemble the quesadillas, put 1 slice of ham on 4 of the tortillas. Sprinkle each with a quarter of the cheese and spoon over a quarter of the baked beans, then top with another tortilla.

Heat the oil in a non-stick frying pan/skillet over medium heat. When hot, add a quesadilla, lower the heat and cook for 2–3 minutes until golden on one side and the cheese begins to melt. Turn over and cook the other side for 2–3 minutes. Transfer to a heatproof plate and keep warm in the preheated oven while you cook the rest.

Melt 1 tablespoon of the butter in a small non-stick frying pan/skillet. Add 1 egg and fry until cooked through, turning once to cook both sides if desired. Repeat to cook the remaining eggs.

To serve, top each quesadilla with a fried egg. Cut into wedges and serve immediately.

SERVES 4–6

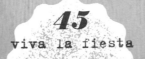

These spicy beef quesadillas are real crowd pleaser — perfect fuel for a late night study session with your classmates.

pepper beef
QUESADILLAS

2 tablespoons vegetable oil

1 onion, diced

1 red (bell) pepper, diced

1 yellow (bell) pepper, diced

1 teaspoon ground cumin

1 teaspoon dried oregano

½ teaspoon paprika

1 fresh red or green chilli/chile, chopped

2 garlic cloves, crushed

450 g/1 lb. minced/ground beef

1 teaspoon sea salt

220 g/1 cup canned chopped tomatoes

8 large flour tortillas

150 g/1½ cups grated Cheddar or Monterey Jack

To serve

sour cream

spring onions/scallions, sliced

diced tomatoes

pitted black olives, sliced

ready-made salsa

SERVES 4–6

Preheat the oven to 120°C (250°F) Gas ½.

Heat 1 tablespoon of the oil in a frying pan/skillet over medium–high heat. Add the onion and peppers and cook for 5–8 minutes, stirring occasionally, until golden. Add the cumin, oregano, paprika, chilli/chile and garlic and cook for 1 minute more. Add the beef and salt and cook for 5 minutes until browned. Stir in the tomatoes and simmer until slightly reduced and thickened. Taste and adjust the seasoning.

To assemble the quesadillas, spread a quarter of the beef mixture on 4 of the tortillas. Sprinkle each with a quarter of the cheese and top with another tortilla.

Heat the remaining oil in a non-stick frying pan/skillet set over medium heat. When hot, add a quesadilla, lower the heat and cook for 2–3 minutes until golden on one side and the cheese begins to melt. Turn over and cook the other side for 2–3 minutes. Transfer to a heatproof plate and keep warm in the oven while you cook the rest.

To serve, top each quesadilla with sour cream, spring onions/scallions, diced tomatoes and sliced olives. Cut into wedges and serve immediately with ready-made salsa on the side.

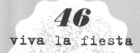

These delicious and filling burritos are fantastic eaten at any time of day, but make sure you're hungry or you won't be able to finish them!

bean & cheese
BURRITOS

2 tablespoons vegetable oil

1 large onion

2 teaspoons ground cumin

2 teaspoons dried oregano

3 garlic cloves, finely chopped

1–2 fresh red chillies/chiles, finely chopped

2 x 400-g/14-oz. cans black beans, drained

1 x 230-g/8-oz. can chopped tomatoes

250 ml/1 cup chicken or vegetable stock, or water

2 teaspoons sea salt

a pinch of sugar

200g/1 cup cooked rice

4–6 large flour tortillas

180 g/scant 2 cups grated Cheddar or Monterey Jack

sprigs of fresh coriander/cilantro, to serve

black pepper

Preheat the oven to 200°C (400°F) Gas 6.

Heat the oil in a large saucepan over medium–high heat. Add the onion, cumin and oregano and cook for 5–8 minutes, stirring occasionally, until golden. Add the garlic and chillies/chiles and cook, stirring often, for 1 minute.

Add the beans, tomatoes, stock or water, salt and sugar and mix well. Bring to the boil and simmer over low heat for 10–15 minutes. Stir in the rice and heat through, then taste and adjust the seasoning.

Divide the bean mixture between the tortillas and sprinkle with grated cheese. Fold in the sides of each tortilla to cover the filling, then roll up to enclose. Place the filled tortillas seam-side down on a greased baking sheet or in a shallow dish. Cover with foil and bake in the preheated oven for 10–15 minutes just to warm through and melt the cheese. Serve hot, topped with sprigs of fresh coriander/cilantro.

SERVES 4–6

The name of this fiery pasta sauce comes from the Italian word arrabiato, meaning angry. For extra spice add some dried chilli/hot pepper flakes.

ULTIMATE ARRABIATA
pasta sauce

60 ml/4 tablespoons olive oil

2 garlic cloves, bruised and skin on

2 tablespoons red wine

500 g/2¼ cups canned chopped tomatoes

1 fresh red chilli/chile, cut lengthways and deseeded

sprig of fresh rosemary

1 bay leaf

½ teaspoon dried oregano

8–10 fresh basil leaves, torn, plus extra to serve

sea salt and black pepper

cooked penne or spaghetti, to serve

grated cheese, to serve

Heat the oil in a saucepan over medium heat and fry the garlic for a few seconds, then add the wine. Cook for about 30 seconds, then add the chopped tomatoes. Add the chilli/chile, rosemary, bay leaf, oregano and ½ teaspoon salt, stir and turn the heat down to low. Cover with a lid and simmer gently for 40–45 minutes.

Taste and adjust the seasoning and when the sauce is spicy enough, discard the chilli/chile. Add a splash of water if the sauce is becoming too dry in the pan. Once cooked, stir in the basil and discard the garlic cloves.

Serve hot with cooked spaghetti or penne and grated cheese, if liked.

SERVES 2

ITALIAN STALLION

This authentic Italian pasta dish is quick to make and very satisfying. A great recipe for a date night at home, it is best enjoyed with a glass of red wine and good company.

PUTTANESCA
pasta sauce

50 g/1¾ oz. anchovy fillets in brine or olive oil, drained

3 tablespoons olive oil

2 garlic cloves, thinly sliced

1 fresh red chilli/chile, deseeded and finely chopped

500 g/2¼ cups canned chopped tomatoes

50 g/⅓ cup capers

40 g/¼ cup pitted green olives, chopped

2 tablespoons tomato purée/paste

100 g/⅔ cup pitted black olives, chopped

sea salt and black pepper

cooked spaghetti, to serve

grated cheese, to serve

Rinse the anchovy fillets under cold water for a few moments to remove excess oil. Pat dry on some kitchen paper/paper towels and chop roughly.

Heat the oil in a saucepan and fry the garlic and chilli/chile for about 3–4 minutes, stirring, until they start to brown. Add the anchovies and continue to cook for about 1 minute, or until they begin to break down. Add the chopped tomatoes, capers, green olives and tomato purée/paste. Stir thoroughly. Turn the heat down and allow to simmer gently, uncovered, for 20 minutes.

Add the black olives and cook for a further 5 minutes. Taste and adjust the seasoning, if necessary. This recipe might not need much salt as the anchovies and the capers are quite salty already.

Serve hot with cooked spaghetti, grated cheese and mixed salad, if liked.

SERVES 2

53
italian stallion

An easy dish made with freezer staples such as grilled pepper slices. These are fantastic for stirring into anything that needs a quick lift.

RAVIOLI BAKE
with grilled sweet peppers

2 tablespoons olive oil

1 onion, halved and sliced

225 g/1⅛ cups frozen sliced grilled peppers

3 garlic cloves, crushed

1 teaspoon dried thyme

¼–½ teaspoon dried chilli/hot pepper flakes, to taste

2 x 400-g/14-oz. cans chopped tomatoes

a pinch of sugar

a large handful of fresh basil or flat-leaf parsley leaves, chopped

500 g/5½ cups small filled ravioli

75 g/¾ cup grated Cheddar

2 tablespoons freshly grated Parmesan

a green salad, to serve (optional)

sea salt and black pepper

Preheat the oven to 200°C (400°F) Gas 6.

Heat the oil in a large saucepan. Add the onion and cook over low heat for 3–5 minutes, until softened. Add the peppers, garlic, thyme and dried chilli/hot pepper flakes and cook, stirring, for 2–3 minutes. Stir in the tomatoes and sugar, season and simmer, uncovered, for 15 minutes. Taste and adjust the seasoning. Stir in the basil.

Cook the ravioli according to the package instructions and drain well.

Tip the cooked ravioli into the sauce and stir gently to coat. Transfer to a greased baking dish, spread evenly and sprinkle both the cheeses over the top.

Bake in the preheated oven for 20–30 minutes, until the cheese is melted and golden. Serve immediately with a green salad, if liked.

SERVES 4–6

Perfect to enjoy with friends while watching movies on a Saturday night, these pizzas are fun to make and cheaper than going to a restaurant. You can add any topping of your preference.

ham & pineapple
PIZZAS

2 ready-made pizza bases 30 cm/12 inches diameter

8 tablespoons passata/Italian sieved tomatoes

4 slices ham, chopped

225 g/1 cup canned pineapple chunks in fruit juice, drained

200 g/7 oz. mozzarella, sliced

Turn the oven on to 200°C (400°F) Gas 6.

Put the pizza bases onto two greased baking sheets. Spread half the tomato passata over the bases with the back of a spoon.

Scatter the ham and pineapple over the pizzas and top with the mozzarella. Bake in the preheated oven for 15–20 minutes or until the bases are cooked. Serve immediately.

MAKES 2

As well as these suggestions, you could serve these pizzas with any toppings you like. Ham, mushrooms and different cheeses all work well.

PIZZETTE
with assorted toppings

4 tablespoons olive or vegetable oil

1 small aubergine/eggplant, thinly sliced

1 onion, thinly sliced

1 teaspoon freshly chopped thyme leaves

4 ready-made pizza bases 15 cm/ 6 inches diameter

4 generous teaspoons tomato purée/paste

75 g/½ cup cherry tomatoes, quartered

125 g/4 oz. blue cheese, crumbled

8 slices of pepperoni

a handful of black olives

100 g/3½ oz. mozzarella, sliced

2 teaspoons basil pesto

2 canned artichoke hearts, sliced

2 tablespoons semi-dried tomatoes

a handful of rocket/arugula

sea salt and black pepper

fresh basil leaves, to garnish

Heat 2 tablespoons of the oil in a frying pan/skillet and fry the aubergine/eggplant on both sides until golden, then remove from the heat. In another pan, heat the remaining oil and gently fry the onion until soft and golden. Add the thyme and remove from the heat.

Preheat the oven to 230°C (450°F) Gas 8.

Put the pizza bases on a baking sheet, then spread 2 of them with tomato purée/paste. Top one pizza with the aubergine/eggplant slices, cherry tomatoes and half the crumbled blue cheese. Top the other pizza with pepperoni, olives and half the mozzarella.

For the third pizza, spread the basil pesto over the base and arrange the artichoke hearts and semi-dried tomatoes on top. Scatter the remaining mozzarella over it. Garnish with basil leaves. Top the last pizza with the sautéed onions and the remaining blue cheese. Season all the pizzas well with salt and pepper and cook on the top shelf of the preheated oven for about 5 minutes, or until golden. Top the onion pizza with the rocket/arugula and serve immediately.

MAKES 4

In this recipe, the beef is cooked slowly with spices and peas resulting in a tasty curry — perfect served with steamed basmati rice or bread.

beef & pea CURRY

2 tablespoons sunflower or vegetable oil

1 large onion, finely chopped

3 garlic cloves, crushed

1 teaspoon finely grated fresh ginger

2–4 fresh green chillies/chiles, thinly sliced

1 tablespoon cumin seeds

3 tablespoons medium curry paste

800 g/1 lb. 12 oz. minced/ground beef

1 x 400-g/14-oz. can chopped tomatoes

1 teaspoon sugar

4 tablespoons tomato purée/paste

4 tablespoons coconut cream

250 g/9 oz. frozen or fresh peas

sea salt and black pepper

a large handful of fresh coriander/cilantro leaves, chopped, to garnish

steamed basmati rice or bread, to serve

SERVES 4

Heat the oil in a large, heavy-based saucepan and add the onion. Cook over low heat for 15–20 minutes, until softened and just turning golden. Add the garlic, ginger, chillies/chiles, cumin seeds and curry paste and stir-fry over high heat for 1–2 minutes.

Add the beef and stir-fry for 3–4 minutes, then stir in the tomatoes, sugar and tomato purée/paste and bring to the boil. Season well, cover and reduce the heat to low. Cook for 1–1½ hours. Add the coconut cream and peas 10 minutes before the end of the cooking time

To serve, garnish with the coriander/cilantro and serve with steamed basmati rice or bread.

SPICE UP YOUR LIFE

Why go out to eat when you can make delicious curries at home? Serve this rich and moreish dish with warm naan bread to mop up the tasty sauce.

BUTTER CHICKEN

800 g/1 lb. 12 oz. boneless, skinless chicken thighs, cut into large bite-sized pieces

50 g/4 tablespoons butter

1 large onion, finely chopped

1 teaspoon ground cinnamon

1 teaspoon ground cardamom

1 teaspoon mild or medium chilli/chili powder

1 x 400-g/14-oz. can chopped tomatoes

150 ml/⅔ cup chicken stock

100 ml/scant ½ cup single/light cream

sea salt and black pepper

freshly chopped coriander/cilantro, to garnish

steamed basmati rice or naan, to serve

Marinade

150 g/1 cup cashew nuts, ground

4 garlic cloves, crushed

4 tablespoons Tandoori curry paste

1 tablespoon vegetable oil

150 g/⅔ cup plain yogurt

To make the marinade, put the cashews, garlic, curry paste, oil and yogurt in a mixing bowl. Stir in the chicken, cover and refrigerate for 1–2 hours.

Melt the butter in a large, non-stick wok or saucepan and add the onion, cinnamon and cardamom. Stir-fry over medium heat for 6–8 minutes, or until the onion has softened. Add the marinated chicken (discarding the marinade) and cook, stirring, for 10 minutes. Season with salt and pepper.

Stir in the chilli/chili powder, tomatoes and stock, bring to the boil, then reduce the heat to low. Simmer, uncovered, for 40–45 minutes, stirring occasionally.

Add the cream and cook gently for a further 4–5 minutes. Garnish with the coriander/cilantro and serve immediately with steamed basmati rice or naan.

SERVES 4

Paneer is an Indian cow's milk cheese easily found in Asian stores. Here it is paired with spinach and tomato to make this colourful vegetable curry.

SAAG PANEER

500 g/1 lb. frozen spinach

50 g/4 tablespoons butter

2 teaspoons cumin seeds

1 onion, finely chopped

2 tomatoes, finely chopped

2 garlic cloves, crushed

1 tablespoon finely grated fresh ginger

1 teaspoon chilli/chili powder

1 teaspoon ground coriander

250 g/8 oz. paneer, cut into bite-sized pieces

2 tablespoons double/heavy cream

2 tablespoons freshly chopped coriander/cilantro

1 teaspoon freshly squeezed lemon juice

sea salt and black pepper

steamed basmati rice or naan, to serve

Bring a large saucepan of water to the boil. Add the frozen spinach and bring back to the boil. Cook for 2–3 minutes, then drain thoroughly. Transfer to a food processor and blend until smooth.

Heat the butter in a large, heavy-based frying pan/skillet. Add the cumin seeds and onion and stir-fry for 6–8 minutes over medium–low heat until the onion turns golden. Add the tomatoes, garlic, ginger, chilli/chili powder and ground coriander. Season well. Stir-fry for 2–3 minutes. Add the paneer and cook for 30–40 seconds over high heat. Add the blended spinach and stir-fry for 4–5 minutes. Stir in the cream, fresh coriander/cilantro and lemon juice. Serve immediately with steamed basmati rice or naan.

SERVES 4

Serve this hearty chickpea curry on its own with steamed basmati rice, or with the spinach and paneer curry on page 64 for a veggie curry feast!

CHICKPEA MASALA

4 tablespoons sunflower oil

4 garlic cloves, crushed

2 teaspoons finely grated fresh ginger

1 large onion, coarsely grated

1–2 fresh green chillies/chiles, thinly sliced

1 teaspoon hot chilli/chili powder, plus extra to garnish

1 tablespoon ground cumin

1 tablespoon ground coriander

3 tablespoons plain yogurt, plus extra, to drizzle

2 teaspoons garam masala

2 teaspoons tamarind paste

2 teaspoons medium curry powder

2 x 400-g/14-oz. cans chickpeas, drained and rinsed

freshly chopped coriander/cilantro leaves, to garnish

steamed basmati rice and lemon wedges, to serve

Heat the sunflower oil in a large, heavy-based frying pan/skillet over medium heat and add the garlic, ginger, onion and chillies/chiles. Stir-fry for 6–8 minutes, or until the onion is golden. Add the chilli/chili powder, cumin, ground coriander, yogurt and garam masala and stir-fry for 1–2 minutes.

Stir in 500 ml/2 cups water and bring to the boil. Add the tamarind paste, curry powder and chickpeas and bring back to the boil. Reduce the heat to low and simmer gently for 30–40 minutes, stirring occasionally, or until the liquid has reduced, coating the chickpeas in a dark, rich sauce.

Serve immediately drizzled with yogurt, garnished with chopped coriander/cilantro and chilli/chili powder, with steamed basmati rice and lemon wedges on the side.

SERVES 4

A spiced oil called 'tarka' is used in this curry to give the dish its distinctive flavour.

This simple yet scrumptious dish is a staple food across India. Serve with bread and pickles.

TARKA DAL

250 g/1¼ cups dried red split lentils

1 teaspoon ground turmeric

4 ripe tomatoes, roughly chopped

6–8 tablespoons freshly chopped coriander/cilantro leaves

Tarka

4 tablespoons sunflower oil

2 teaspoons black mustard seeds

3 teaspoons cumin seeds

2 garlic cloves, very thinly sliced

2 teaspoons very finely chopped fresh ginger

6–8 fresh curry leaves

1 dried red chilli/chile

2 teaspoons ground cumin

2 teaspoons ground coriander

sea salt and black pepper

Rinse the lentils until the water runs clear. Put them in a heavy-based saucepan with 1 litre/4 cups water. Bring to the boil over high heat, skimming off any scum that rises to the surface. Lower the heat and cook for 20–25 minutes. Remove from the heat and using a hand-held blender or whisk, blend until smooth. Return to the heat and stir in the turmeric and tomatoes. Bring to the boil, season and stir in the coriander/cilantro. To make the tarka, heat the sunflower oil in a frying pan/skillet. Add all the ingredients and stir-fry for 1–2 minutes. Stir into the dal and serve immediately.

SPINACH DAL

120 g/⅔ cup dried black lentils

45 g/3 tablespoons butter

1 onion, finely chopped

3 garlic cloves, crushed

2 teaspoons finely grated fresh ginger

2 fresh green chillies/chiles, halved lengthways

1 teaspoon ground turmeric

1 teaspoon paprika

1 tablespoon ground coriander

1 tablespoon ground cumin

200 g/7 oz. canned red kidney beans, drained

200 g/7 oz. spinach

a handful of fresh coriander/cilantro, chopped

150 ml/⅔ cup double/heavy cream

Rinse the lentils. Drain, place in a deep bowl and cover with cold water. Leave to soak for 10–12 hours. Rinse the lentils, then place in a saucepan with 500 ml/2 cups boiling water. Bring to the boil, reduce the heat and simmer for 35–40 minutes, or until tender. Drain and set aside. Melt the butter in a saucepan and stir-fry the onion, garlic, ginger and chillies/chiles for 5–6 minutes, then add the turmeric, paprika, ground coriander, cumin, kidney beans and lentils. Add 500 ml/2 cups water and bring to the boil. Reduce the heat and stir in the spinach. Cook gently for 10–15 minutes, stirring often. Stir in the coriander/cilantro and cream. Serve immediately.

BOTH SERVE 4

These crispy falafels are delicious served with hummus, toasted flatbreads and pickled chilli/chile peppers.

HERBY FALAFEL
with hummus & toasted flatbreads

200 g/1 cup dried chickpeas

100 g/1 cup broad/fava beans

2 garlic cloves, crushed

2 tablespoons freshly chopped coriander/cilantro

2 tablespoons freshly chopped flat-leaf parsley

2 tablespoons freshly chopped mint

1 shallot, finely chopped

1 teaspoon ground cumin

1 teaspoon ground coriander

½ teaspoon ground cayenne pepper

1 teaspoon bicarbonate of soda/baking soda

freshly squeezed juice of 1 lemon

2 tablespoons sesame seeds

sea salt and black pepper

about 1 litre/4 cups sunflower oil, for deep-frying

ready-made hummus, toasted flatbreads and pickled green chilli/chile peppers, to serve

Soak the dried chickpeas overnight in a large bowl of cold water. The next day, drain and rinse the chickpeas. Bring a saucepan of water to the boil, add half the chickpeas and cook for about 15–20 minutes, or until tender. Add the broad/fava beans and cook for a further 2 minutes. Drain and tip into the bowl of a food processor with the remaining uncooked, soaked chickpeas.

Add the garlic, chopped herbs, shallot, spices, bicarbonate of soda/baking soda, lemon juice and 1 teaspoon salt. Season with black pepper and whiz until almost smooth.

Tip the mixture into a bowl and roll into 12 even-sized balls, then flatten slightly to make patties. Press the sesame seeds into both sides of each falafel.

Fill a deep-fat fryer with sunflower oil or pour oil to a depth of about 4 cm/1½ inches into a deep saucepan. Heat until a cube of bread sizzles and browns in about 5 seconds. Cook the falafel in batches of 3–4 at a time in the hot fat until golden brown. Drain on kitchen paper/paper towels.

Serve the falafel with the red pepper hummus, toasted flatbreads, and pickled green chilli/chile peppers.

SERVES 4

VEGGIE MIGHTY

These spicy veggie pancakes are made with chickpea flour (also called gram flour). It is available in most health food stores.

carrot & chickpea
PANCAKES

8–10 tomatoes

2 tablespoons olive oil, plus extra for drizzling

1 tablespoon fresh thyme leaves

125 g/scant 1 cup grated courgette/zucchini

125 g/1 cup grated carrot

1 garlic clove, crushed

1 tablespoon freshly chopped coriander/cilantro

1 tablespoon freshly chopped mint

½ teaspoon ground cumin

½ teaspoon ground coriander

¼ teaspoon cayenne pepper

125 g/1 cup chickpea flour

½ teaspoon baking powder

100 g/⅔ cup crumbled feta

100 ml/½ cup milk

1 egg, lightly beaten

sea salt and black pepper

1 tablespoon sunflower oil

ready-made hummus and baby salad leaves, to serve

Preheat the oven to 170°C (325°F) Gas 3.

Cut the tomatoes in half, arrange on a small baking sheet, cut-side up, and drizzle with 2 tablespoons of olive oil. Scatter over the thyme and season with salt and pepper. Roast in the oven for 30–40 minutes until soft and starting to brown. Remove from the oven and let cool.

To make the pancakes, tip the courgette/zucchini, carrot, garlic, herbs, spices, flour and baking powder into a mixing bowl and stir until combined. Add the feta, milk and egg and mix into a batter. Season with salt and pepper.

Heat half the sunflower oil in a frying pan/skillet. Add 4 tablespoons of the batter to the pan in separate dollops. Cook over low–medium heat for about 2 minutes, or until golden brown on the underside. Carefully flip the pancakes over and cook the other side until golden. Remove from the pan and keep warm while you cook the remaining batter, adding more oil to the pan, if needed.

Arrange the pancakes on serving plates with a spoonful of hummus, a few roasted tomatoes and baby salad leaves and drizzle with olive oil. Serve warm.

SERVES 2

This recipe can also be made as small pasties. Cut out pastry circles with a cookie cutter, fill with vegetable mixture, fold over, seal and bake.

VEGETABLE PIE

Tomato sauce

1 small onion, chopped

1 celery stalk, chopped

1–2 tablespoons olive oil

2 garlic cloves, finely chopped

1 teaspoon sea salt

a splash of wine (optional)

225-g/8-oz. can chopped tomatoes

a pinch of sugar

2 sheets ready-made puff pastry

3–4 large mushrooms, sliced

1 yellow (bell) pepper, diced

200 g/1 cup (sweet) corn kernels

150-g/5-oz. canned borlotti, cannellini or pinto beans, drained

75 g/3 cups fresh spinach leaves, washed and dried (optional)

80 g/⅔ cup grated Cheddar

2–3 tablespoons milk, for glazing

To make the tomato sauce, combine the onion, celery and oil in a frying pan/skillet and cook until soft. Add the garlic and cook for 1 minute. Season with salt and add the wine, if using. Stir and cook until evaporated. Add the tomatoes and sugar and stir. Cook for at least 15 minutes. Taste and adjust the seasoning and set aside until needed.

Preheat the oven to 200°C (400°F) Gas 6.

Line a baking sheet with one of the pastry sheets, leaving at least 1-cm/½-inch overhang on all sides. Spread with the tomato sauce in an even layer. Arrange the mushrooms, pepper, corn, beans, spinach, if using, and cheese on top of the sauce.

Cover with the remaining pastry sheet, fold the bottom edge over and push down to seal. Brush the top with milk to glaze. Cut a series of slits in the top starting in one corner and working across, to allow steam to escape.

Bake in the preheated oven for 25–30 minutes, until browned. Serve warm with boiled or steamed new potatoes and a salad, if liked.

SERVES 4–6

This colourful salad with its herby pesto dressing is perfect for a summer evening meal. Feel free to use feta instead of goat cheese if you prefer.

ROASTED VEGETABLE SALAD
with herby goat cheese

4 small–medium beetroot/beets

½ medium butternut squash, deseeded and cut into wedges

2 garlic cloves, unpeeled

1 tablespoon fresh thyme leaves

4 tablespoons olive oil

1 red onion, cut into wedges

1 red (bell) pepper, cut into chunks

6 spring onions/scallions, trimmed

a handful of mixed salad leaves

150 g/5 oz. mild soft goat cheese

sea salt and black pepper

Dressing

4 tablespoons olive oil

1 tablespoon ready-made pesto

1 tablespoon white wine vinegar

Preheat the oven to 170°C (325°F) Gas 3.

Arrange the beetroot/beets in a roasting dish and cover tightly with foil. Roast in the oven for about 1 hour, or until tender. Remove the foil and let cool.

Turn the oven up to 200°C (400°F) Gas 6.

Arrange the butternut squash on a baking sheet with the garlic cloves and thyme. Drizzle with the oil, season with salt and pepper and roast in the oven for 15 minutes.

Add the onion, pepper and spring onions/scallions to the squash and continue to cook for 20 minutes, or until tender. Remove from the oven and let cool.

While the vegetables are roasting, make the dressing. Put the oil, pesto and vinegar in a jar with a lid and shake until blended. Taste and adjust the seasoning.

Peel the skin from the roasted beetroot/beets and cut into wedges. Arrange all the roasted vegetables on a serving plate with the salad leaves. Crumble the goat cheese and scatter over the top. Drizzle the dressing over the salad and serve immediately.

SERVES 4–6

Quinoa is high in protein, calcium and iron; combining it with beans and dried fruit here makes a winning recovery meal.

fruity quinoa &
BEAN STEW

200 g/1 cup red split lentils

100 g/⅔ cup quinoa

1 teaspoon Baharat spice blend or Ras el Hanout

1 tablespoon olive oil

2 onions, chopped

6 garlic cloves, crushed

2 x 400-g/14-oz. cans chopped tomatoes

600 ml/2½ cups good vegetable stock

3 tablespoons hot sauce

2 bay leaves

1 sprig of fresh thyme

75 g/½ cup chopped dried apricots

75 g/½ cup sultanas/golden raisins

1–2 fresh red chillies/chiles, chopped

2 x 400-g/14-oz. cans mixed beans, drained

1 x 400-g/14-oz. can chickpeas, drained

2 red (bell) peppers, deseeded and sliced

sea salt and black pepper

cooked couscous or brown rice, to serve

Rinse the lentils and quinoa and put them in a saucepan of boiling water.

Reduce the heat to a gentle simmer and add the Baharat spice blend. Cook, uncovered, for 20 minutes, or until thick. Drain well.

Heat the oil in a stovetop casserole dish and gently fry the onions and garlic until softened but not brown.

Add the chopped tomatoes and the cooked lentils and quinoa. Stir well.

Add the vegetable stock and bring back to a simmer.

Add the hot sauce, bay leaves, thyme, apricots, sultanas/golden raisins, chillies/chiles, mixed beans, chickpeas and peppers. Stir well. Bring to the boil, then reduce the heat to a very gentle simmer and cook, covered, for at least 1 hour. Stir occasionally.

Add more stock if it looks too dry, but allow the sauce to thicken. Taste and season with salt and pepper.

Serve immediately with couscous or brown rice.

GYM JOCKS v YOGA BUNNIES

This uncomplicated salad makes a great pre- or post- workout lunch. Serve with fresh bread for a well-balanced and filling meal.

tuna & cannellini
BEAN SALAD

1 red onion, thinly sliced

1 x 175-g/6-oz. can tuna, drained

1 x 400-g/14-oz. can cannellini beans, drained and rinsed

a large bunch of fresh flat-leaf parsley, chopped

freshly squeezed juice of 1 lemon

4 tablespoons olive oil

sea salt and black pepper

fresh bread, to serve

Put the onion, tuna, cannellini beans and parsley in a large serving bowl. Add the lemon juice and oil and toss gently to combine.

Season to taste with salt and pepper. Serve with plenty of fresh bread.

SERVES 2–3

Barley is a high-fibre, high-protein grain. In this recipe, it is used instead of rice to make a healthy and satisfying risotto.

BARLEY RISOTTO
with carrots

1.5 litres/6 cups vegetable stock

1 onion, diced

2–3 carrots, diced

2 tablespoons olive or vegetable oil

300 g/1½ cups barley

a handful of freshly chopped flat-leaf parsley (optional)

sea salt and black pepper

finely grated cheese, to serve (optional)

Put the stock in a saucepan and bring just to a simmer.

Combine the onion, carrots and oil in a separate saucepan and cook for 3–5 minutes, until soft. Add the barley and cook for 1 minute, stirring to coat. Season lightly. Add 2 ladlefuls of stock to the barley and cook, stirring constantly, until the liquid is absorbed. Continue adding the stock a ladleful at a time and stirring for about 30–40 minutes, until the barley is tender and most, if not all, of the stock has gone. Taste and adjust the seasoning.

Stir in the parsley, if using, and serve immediately with finely grated cheese, if liked.

SERVES 4–6

Adding high-protein grains such as barley to this traditional Greek salad makes it a hearty meal in itself. Quinoa could also be used if you prefer.

Greek barley
SALAD

100 g/½ cup barley

freshly squeezed juice and finely grated zest of 1 lemon

2 teaspoons white or red wine vinegar

4 tablespoons olive oil

1 red onion, thinly sliced

4 tomatoes, chopped

1 large cucumber, chopped

1 green (bell) pepper, deseeded and chopped

20 pitted black olives (optional)

150 g/5 oz. feta

1 teaspoon dried oregano

sea salt and black pepper

Cook the barley in a saucepan of boiling salted water for 30 minutes or until tender. Drain and set aside.

In a large serving bowl, whisk together the lemon juice and zest, vinegar and oil, then stir in the warm barley and mix well. Let cool.

Add the onion to the barley along with the tomatoes, cucumber, green pepper and olives, if using, and mix to combine. Season to taste with salt and pepper.

Crumble the feta over the top of the salad and sprinkle with oregano. Serve immediately.

SERVES 4

Tofu is high in protein and low in fat and these delicious skewers prove that you don't have to miss out on taste to eat healthily!

SPICY TOFU SKEWERS
with soy dipping sauce

300 g/10½ oz. tofu, rinsed, drained and cubed

leaves from a small bunch of fresh basil, shredded, to serve

sesame oil, for frying

Marinade

3 lemongrass stalks, trimmed and finely chopped

1 tablespoon vegetable oil

3 tablespoons soy sauce

1–2 fresh red chillies/chiles, deseeded and finely chopped

2 garlic cloves, crushed

1 teaspoon ground turmeric

2 teaspoons sugar

sea salt

Soy dipping sauce

4–5 tablespoons soy sauce

1–2 tablespoons Thai fish sauce

freshly squeezed juice of 1 lime

1–2 teaspoons sugar

1 fresh red chilli/chile, deseeded and finely chopped

a packet of wooden or bamboo skewers, soaked in water before use

To make the marinade, mix the lemongrass, oil, soy sauce, chilli/chile, garlic and turmeric with the sugar until it has dissolved. Add the tofu, season with salt and toss to coat. Leave to marinate for 1 hour.

Prepare the soy dipping sauce by whisking all the ingredients together. Set aside until ready to serve.

To cook the tofu, stir-fry the cubes in a wok with a little sesame oil and then thread them onto sticks to serve, or skewer them and grill them on the barbecue or under a conventional grill/broiler for 2–3 minutes on each side. Serve the tofu hot, garnished with the shredded basil and with the dipping sauce on the side.

SERVES 3–4

Satay sauce goes perfectly with these spicy beef skewers. It is best to make your own but a ready-made verison can be found in most Asian stores.

FIERY BEEF SKEWERS
with satay sauce

500 g/1 lb. beef steak, sliced into bite-sized pieces

1 tablespoon peanut oil

Satay sauce

60 ml/¼ cup vegetable oil

4–5 garlic cloves, crushed

1 tablespoon dried chilli/hot pepper flakes

1–2 teaspoons curry powder

60 g/½ cup roasted peanuts, finely ground

To serve

a small bunch of fresh coriander/cilantro (optional)

a small bunch of fresh mint (optional)

lime wedges (optional)

a packet of short wooden or bamboos skewers, soaked in water before use

To make the sauce, heat the oil in a heavy-based saucepan and stir in the garlic until it begins to colour. Add the chillies/chiles, curry powder and the peanuts and stir over low heat, until the mixture forms a paste. Remove from the heat and let cool.

Put the beef pieces in a bowl. Stir the oil into the sauce and tip the mixture onto the beef. Mix well, so that the beef is evenly coated and thread the meat onto the skewers.

Prepare the barbecue or preheat the grill/broiler to hot. Cook the skewers for 2–3 minutes on each side, then serve immediately with the fresh herbs and lime wedges.

SERVES 4–6

CHILL WHILE YOU GRILL

This is a great way to enjoy pumpkin. Serve these spicy wedges on their own or with any grilled, roasted or barbecued meat.

ROASTED PUMPKIN WEDGES
with lime & spices

1 medium-sized pumpkin, halved lengthways, deseeded and cut into 6–8 segments

2 teaspoons coriander seeds

1 teaspoon cumin seeds

1 teaspoon fennel seeds

1–2 teaspoons ground cinnamon

2 teaspoons dried chilli/hot pepper flakes

2 garlic cloves

2 tablespoons olive oil

coarse sea salt

finely grated zest of 1 lime

6 wooden or metal skewers, to serve (optional)

Preheat the oven to 200°C (400°F) Gas 6 or prepare the barbecue.

Using a mortar and pestle, grind all the dried spices with the salt.

Add the garlic and a little of the olive oil to form a paste. Rub the mixture over the pumpkin wedges and put them, skin-side down, in a baking dish or roasting pan. Cook them in the preheated oven for 35–40 minutes, or barbecue until tender. Sprinkle over the lime zest and serve hot, threaded onto skewers, if using.

SERVES 6

When it's warm outside, what could be better than getting a few friends together for a barbecue? These chicken skewers are guaranteed to please.

CHICKEN TANDOORI
skewers

1 kg/2¼ lbs. chicken breasts, cut into bite-sized pieces

30 g/2 tablespoons butter, melted

Marinade

3 fresh red or green chillies/chiles, deseeded and chopped

2–3 garlic cloves, chopped

2 tablespoons finely chopped fresh ginger

2 tablespoons double/heavy cream

3 tablespoons vegetable oil

1 tablespoon paprika

2 teaspoons ground cumin

2 teaspoons ground cardamom

1 teaspoon ground cloves

1 teaspoon sea salt

To serve

crispy poppadoms

tomato, cucumber and onion salad

limes wedges

4–6 long, thin metal skewers

To prepare the marinade, use a mortar and pestle, or an electric blender, to blend the chillies/chiles, garlic and ginger to a paste. Beat in the cream and oil with 3–4 tablespoons water to form a smooth mixture. Beat in the dried spices.

Put the chicken pieces in a bowl and rub with the marinade until thoroughly coated. Cover and chill in the refrigerator for at least 1 hour. Lift the chicken pieces out of the marinade and thread them onto the skewers.

Prepare a barbecue or preheat the grill/broiler to medium–hot. Brush the chicken with the melted butter and cook for 3–4 minutes. Serve immediately with crispy poppadoms, a salad of finely diced tomato, cucumber and onion with fresh coriander/cilantro, and wedges of lime for squeezing, if liked.

SERVES 4–6

Serve these vibrant veggie skewers with warm pita breads and a good spoonful of the herby tapenade. They are best eaten immediately after cooking.

CHARGRILLED HALLOUMI
with mixed olive & herb tapenade

250 g/8 oz. halloumi, cut into chunks

1 red (bell) pepper, deseeded and cut into chunks

1 courgette/zucchini

1 teaspoon coriander seeds

1 teaspoon cumin seeds

1 garlic clove, crushed

½ teaspoon dried oregano

2–3 tablespoons olive oil

sea salt and black pepper

toasted pita breads, to serve

Tapenade

4 tablespoons mixed pitted olives

freshly grated zest of ½ lemon

2 tablespoons freshly chopped flat-leaf parsley leaves

1 tablespoon freshly chopped mint leaves

1 garlic clove

4 tablespoons olive oil

8 wooden or bamboo skewers, soaked in water before use

Put the halloumi and red pepper in a shallow dish.

Toast the coriander seeds and cumin seeds in a dry frying pan/skillet over medium heat for about 1 minute, or until aromatic. Crush lightly using a pestle and mortar and add to the halloumi and vegetables. Add the garlic, oregano and olive oil. Season with black pepper, mix well to combine and set aside to marinate for an hour or so.

To make the tapenade, tip all the ingredients into a food processor and whiz until combined and roughly chopped. Taste and add black pepper and salt if necessary, but remember that the halloumi is quite salty already.

Prepare the barbecue or preheat a stovetop griddle/grill pan. Thread the marinated halloumi, courgettes/zucchini and peppers onto the skewers, making sure that each one has an even amount of vegetables and cheese. Cook the skewers in batches until golden and the cheese has softened. Serve with the tapenade and toasted pita breads.

SERVES 4

95

chill while you grill

Peri-peri is a spicy marinade used in East and West Africa. Delicious with grilled chicken and fish, it is perfect for these seafood skewers.

peri-peri
SHRIMP SKEWERS

24 large prawns/shrimp, deveined

Peri-peri

175 g/1½ sticks butter

3–4 garlic cloves, crushed

100 ml/scant ½ cup olive oil

2 tablespoons dried chilli/hot pepper flakes

freshly squeezed juice of 2 lemons

sea salt

a packet of wooden or bamboo skewers, soaked in water before use

To make the peri-peri, melt the butter in a frying pan/skillet and stir in the garlic. Set aside. Heat the olive oil in a separate pan and add the dried chilli/hot pepper flakes. Turn off the heat and leave the oil to cool. When cool, transfer the oil to a mixing bowl and beat in the garlic-flavoured butter, lemon juice and a little salt.

Thread the prawns/shrimp onto the prepared skewers. Brush the prawns/shrimp with the peri-peri butter. Prepare the barbecue or preheat a grill/broiler to medium-hot. Cook the skewers for about 2 minutes on each side, basting them with the peri-peri, until the shells have turned orange. Serve immediately with any remaining peri-peri on the side for dipping.

SERVES 4–6

This quick and easy dish is ideal for impressing your classroom crush! Use Cheddar instead of goat cheese if you prefer – it's just as delicious.

baked, goat cheese-stuffed
CHICKEN BREAST

2 skinless chicken breasts

50 g/2 oz. firm goat cheese, grated

1 fresh red chilli/chile, deseeded and finely chopped

small handful of fresh coriander/cilantro, chopped

1 shallot, very finely chopped

2 large bacon slices

olive oil, for greasing

2 corn cobs

sea salt and black pepper

mixed salad, to serve

cocktail sticks/toothpicks

Preheat the oven to 190°C (375°F) Gas 5.

Take a sharp knife and form a cavity in the side of each of the chicken breasts by cutting lengthways from one end to the other.

In a bowl, combine the cheese, chilli/chile, coriander/cilantro and shallot and mix well. Carefully stuff each chicken breast with the cheese mixture by pressing it into the chicken cavity with a teaspoon. Skewer the open side of each chicken breast with cocktail sticks/toothpicks to prevent the stuffing from escaping. Lightly season each chicken breast with salt and pepper, then wrap a slice of bacon around each one.

Lightly grease the ovenproof frying pan/skillet with olive oil over high heat. Sear the chicken in the pan until golden brown on both sides. Transfer the pan to the preheated oven and cook for 20–25 minutes or until the chicken is thoroughly cooked through.

A few minutes before the chicken has finished cooking, put the corn in a saucepan of boiling salted water, wait for the water to return to the boil, then cook for 2–3 minutes.

Preheat the ridged stovetop grill pan/griddle. Remove the corn from the saucepan and drain. Toss the corn in a tablespoon of olive oil and season with salt and pepper. Lightly char the corn in the hot grill pan/griddle.

SERVES 2

Serve the chicken and corn with a mixed salad.

POSH NOSH

Pies are a wonderful thing. They look and taste fantastic, and are very easy to make. Serve with creamy mashed potatoes and peas, if liked.

STEAK, LEEK & MUSHROOM PIE
with Guinness

1 tablespoon vegetable oil

700 g/1½ lbs. stewing beef, cut into bite-sized pieces

2 trimmed leeks, sliced into rounds

1 onion, coarsely chopped

2 large carrots, peeled and diced

250 g/9 oz. mushrooms, coarsely chopped

3 bacon slices, coarsely chopped

1 teaspoon dried thyme

2 garlic cloves, crushed

2 tablespoons plain/all-purpose flour

1 x 330-ml/12-oz. can Guinness

2 tablespoons Worcestershire sauce

1 bay leaf

a large handful of fresh flat-leaf parsley leaves, chopped

375-g/13-oz. pack ready-rolled puff pastry, defrosted if frozen

melted butter or milk, to brush

sea salt and black pepper

Preheat the oven to 160°C (325°F) Gas 3.

Heat the oil in a large flameproof casserole dish. Add the beef and cook, stirring, for 2–3 minutes, until just browned. Remove the meat from the casserole dish, season and set aside.

Add the leeks, onion and carrots to the pan, adding a little more oil if necessary. Cook over low heat for about 3 minutes, until softened. Add the mushrooms, bacon and thyme and cook for a further 2–3 minutes. Season well. Add the garlic and cook for 1 minute.

Return the beef to the casserole dish, add the flour, stir to coat the meat in the flour and cook for 2–3 minutes. Pour in the Guinness and Worcestershire sauce. Add the bay leaf and parsley and pour in sufficient cold water to just cover. Stir to mix, cover with a lid and bake in the preheated oven for about 1½ hours.

Remove the casserole from the oven and increase the oven temperature to 200°C (400°F) Gas 6.

Transfer the beef mixture to a baking dish. Unroll the pastry and use to cover the pie filling. Fold over the edges and crimp roughly with your fingers. Using a sharp knife, and starting at the top edge, make lengthways slits on the diagonal, in stripes about ½ cm apart, all the way across. Brush with melted butter or milk and bake in the preheated oven for about 25–30 minutes, until golden. Serve immediately with mashed potatoes and peas.

101
POSH NOSH

SERVES 4–6

If smoked fish is difficult to obtain, simply increase the quantity of the others. Serve with peas or wilted fresh spinach.

FISH PIE
with leeks & herbs

1 kg/2¼ lbs. floury potatoes, peeled and chopped

115 g/1 stick butter

about 850 ml/3⅓ cups milk (250 ml/1 cup of which is warmed)

1 tablespoon olive oil

1 trimmed leek, cut into thin rounds

1 bay leaf

2 tablespoons dry white wine

300 g/10 oz. any firm white fish fillet, such as cod

200 g/7 oz. boneless, skinless salmon

150 g/6 oz. undyed smoked haddock

175 g/6 oz. peeled cooked prawns/shrimp

35 g/⅓ cup plain/all-purpose flour

1 teaspoon dry mustard powder

a small bunch of chives, snipped

a large handful of fresh flat-leaf parsley leaves, chopped

sea salt and black pepper

SERVES 6

Put the potatoes in a large saucepan and add sufficient cold water to cover. Season with salt and bring to the boil. Cook until the potatoes are tender, then drain. Mash the potatoes with all but 50 g/3 tablespoons of the butter, the 250 ml/1 cup warmed milk and some salt. Taste and adjust the seasoning. Set aside.

Preheat the oven to 190ºC (375ºF) Gas 5.

Put the oil in a small saucepan and add the leek. Cook for about 5 minutes, until soft. Season lightly, add the wine and cook until the liquid is almost fully reduced. Set aside.

Combine the remaining milk and bay leaf in a large shallow pan and bring to the boil. Add the white fish fillets and poach for about 5 minutes until almost cooked, then set aside. Add the salmon and repeat. Add the haddock and repeat. Transfer the poaching milk to a measuring jug and top up with milk to 600 ml/2½ cups, if necessary.

Melt the remaining butter in a medium saucepan over low heat. Add the flour and cook, whisking, for 1 minute. Slowly pour in the reserved milk, whisking continuously, and simmer until the mixture thickens. Add the mustard and season to taste. Stir in the chives and parsley.

Flake the fish and put it in a greased baking dish. Add the prawns/shrimp and leeks. Pour over the sauce and stir well to mix. Spread evenly. Top with the mashed potatoes and spread in an even layer. Bake in the preheated oven for 35–45 minutes, until browned. Serve immediately.

Be the host with the most and wow your friends with this surprisingly easy bacon and onion tart. Serve with a leafy green side salad.

creamy bacon & onion
TART

1 tablespoon olive oil

170 g/5½ oz. diced bacon

3 onions, sliced

1 garlic clove, crushed

1 teaspoon sugar

2 sprigs of fresh thyme

375 g/12½ oz. ready-rolled puff pastry, defrosted if frozen

250 g/1 cup crème fraîche/sour cream

sea salt and black pepper

Preheat the oven to 200°C (400°F) Gas 6.

Heat the olive oil in a large frying pan/skillet over medium heat, add the bacon and cook until crisp. Remove from the pan with a slotted spoon and drain on kitchen paper/paper towels. Add the sliced onions to the pan and cook for about 10 minutes, stirring occasionally until they start to colour. Add the garlic, sugar and thyme and cook for a further minute to caramelize the onions. Remove from the heat, stir in the bacon and let cool slightly.

Unroll out the puff pastry on a lightly floured work surface. Roll out with a rolling pin until it's big enough to trim into a rectangle about 30 x 20 cm/12 x 8 inches. Using the tip of the knife, score a border 2 cm/1 inch from the edge without cutting all the way through. Carefully lift the pastry onto a baking sheet and slide into the preheated oven. Cook for 7 minutes, then remove from the oven.

Season the crème fraîche/sour cream with salt and pepper and spread half of it over the tart base. Season the onion and bacon mixture with salt and pepper and spread over the crème fraîche/sour cream. Dot the remaining crème fraîche/sour cream over the filling and return to the oven for a further 20 minutes, or until the pastry is golden and the filling is bubbling.

Serve hot or warm with a leafy green salad.

SERVES 4

SERVES 4

This improves over time so is best made a day in advance, refrigerated and baked when ready to serve.

MOUSSAKA

1 onion, chopped

4–5 tablespoons olive oil

500 g/1 lb. minced/ground lamb

2 garlic cloves, finely chopped

½ teaspoon ground allspice

¼ teaspoon ground cinnamon

2 teaspoons dried oregano

125 ml/½ cup red wine

2 x 400-g cans chopped tomatoes

1 bay leaf, plus extra to garnish

a pinch of sugar

3 medium aubergines/eggplant, sliced into 1-cm/½ inch rounds

sea salt and black pepper

Topping

350 ml/1½ cups Greek yogurt

2 eggs, beaten

150 g/6 oz. feta, crumbled

a large handful of fresh mint leaves, chopped

3 tablespoons freshly grated Parmesan

Combine the onion and 1 tablespoon of the oil in a large frying pan/skillet. Cook the onion for about 3–5 minutes, until soft. Add the lamb, season well and cook, stirring, for about 5 minutes, until browned. Add the garlic, allspice, cinnamon and oregano and cook for 1 minute. Add the wine and cook for 1 minute more. Add the tomatoes, bay leaf and sugar and mix well. Let simmer gently, uncovered, while you prepare the aubergines.

Preheat the oven to 200°C (400°F) Gas 6.

Heat the remaining oil in a large non-stick frying pan/skillet. Add the aubergine/eggplant slices in a single layer and cook to brown slightly. Using tongs, turn and cook the other sides, then transfer to kitchen paper/paper towels to drain. Work in batches, adding more oil as necessary, until all the aubergine/eggplant slices are browned.

In a bowl, combine the yogurt, eggs and feta and mix well with a fork until blended. Season well with salt and pepper and stir in the mint. Set aside.

Arrange half of the lamb mixture on the bottom of a greased baking dish. Top with half of the aubergine slices. Repeat once more. Spread the yogurt mixture on top and level the surface. Sprinkle with the Parmesan and decorate with bay leaves.

Bake in the preheated oven for about 40–50 minutes, until golden brown and bubbling. Serve immediately.

Warming, hearty and comforting, meatballs are a home-cooked classic that will transport you back to your mum's kitchen. Serve with mashed potatoes.

CHICKEN MEATBALLS
with roasted onions & tomatoes

3 onions

6 fresh plum tomatoes, quartered

4 tablespoons olive oil

1 teaspoon dried thyme

125 g/1¼ cups mushrooms, coarsely chopped

100 g/3½ oz. ham

a large handful of fresh flat-leaf parsley leaves, chopped

2 garlic cloves, crushed

500 g/1 lb. minced/ground chicken

1 teaspoon paprika

1 egg, beaten

5 tablespoons fresh breadcrumbs

milk, to soften

sea salt and black pepper

Preheat the oven to 200°C (400°F) Gas 6.

Halve 1 of the onions and chop coarsely; set aside. Cut the remaining onions into quarters and toss with 2–3 tablespoons of the oil and the thyme. Arrange the onion quarters and tomatoes on a baking sheet lined with foil. Set aside while you prepare the meatballs.

In a food processor, combine the coarsely chopped onion, mushrooms, ham and parsley. Process until finely chopped. Transfer to a frying pan/skillet and add 1–2 tablespoons of the oil. Cook for 3–5 minutes, until softened. Add the garlic, season well and cook for 1 minute more. Let cool slightly.

In a bowl, combine the chicken, paprika, egg, breadcrumbs and the mushroom mixture. Add a good pinch of salt. Mix well with your hands to combine. The mixture should be quite moist. If it is too dry, soften with milk, adding 1 tablespoon at a time.

Form the chicken mixture into roughly-shaped meatballs, and arrange them on a baking sheet lined with parchment paper. Season the onions and tomatoes and put both of the baking sheets into the preheated oven. Bake for about 35–45 minutes, until the meatballs and vegetables are browned. Serve together.

SERVES 4–6

just like mum used to make

If you're feeling a bit homesick, there's no better remedy than a steaming bowl of hot, creamy pasta to wash those blues away.

tuna noodle
CASSEROLE

2 tablespoons olive oil

3 spring onions/scallions, thinly sliced

1 celery stalk, finely chopped

100 g/1 cup sliced button mushrooms

2 tablespoons capers (optional)

150 g/1½ cups fresh breadcrumbs

a good pinch of paprika

350 g/12 oz. dried egg tagliatelle

45 g/3 tablespoons butter

35 g/⅓ cup plain/all-purpose flour

600 ml/2½ cups hot milk

1 teaspoon mustard powder

1 x 350-g/12-oz. can tuna in oil, drained

a large handful of fresh flat-leaf parsley leaves, chopped

sea salt and black pepper

Preheat the oven to 180°C (350°F) Gas 4.

Heat the oil in a large frying pan/skillet and add the spring onions/scallions, celery and mushrooms. Cook over medium heat for 3–5 minutes, until soft. Season lightly with salt, stir in the capers, if using, and set aside. Season the breadcrumbs and add the paprika. Set aside.

Cook the pasta according to the package instructions. Drain, toss in a little olive oil and set aside.

Melt the butter in a small saucepan set over low heat. Add the flour and cook, stirring, for 1 minute. Gradually pour in the hot milk, whisking constantly, and simmer until the mixture thickens. Stir in the mustard. Let cool slightly. Taste and adjust the seasoning if necessary.

Put the cooked pasta in the prepared baking dish. Pour over the sauce, mushroom mixture, tuna and parsley and toss to mix well. Spread evenly and sprinkle the seasoned breadcrumbs over the top. Bake in the preheated oven for 20–30 minutes, until browned. Serve immediately with a mixed salad.

SERVES 4

III

just like mum used to make

Easy to make and even easier to enjoy, this stew is the perfect one-pot dinner. This recipe makes a big batch so you can freeze half for a rainy day.

SAUSAGE, PASTA & BEAN STEW
with greens

1 tablespoon olive oil

1 large onion, coarsely chopped

12 large sausages cut into bite-sized pieces

4 garlic cloves, sliced

¼–1 teaspoon dried chilli/hot pepper flakes, to taste

1 x 400-g/14-oz. can chopped tomatoes

250 ml/1 cup red wine

1 bay leaf

100 g/1 cup small pasta shapes, such as macaroni

about 175 g/1 cup greens, such as curly kale, chard or cavolo nero

1 x 400-g/14-oz. can cannellini beans, drained

a large handful of fresh basil leaves, chopped

sea salt and black pepper

freshly grated cheese, to serve (optional)

crusty bread, to serve (optional)

Heat the oil in a large saucepan. Add the onion and cook for 3–5 minutes, until soft. Add the sausage and cook for about 5 minutes, until browned. Stir in the garlic and dried chilli/hot pepper flakes and cook for 1 minute.

Add the tomatoes, wine and bay leaf and enough water to cover. Don't worry if it's soupy at this stage. Bring to the boil, then add the pasta and cook, uncovered, for about 10 minutes, until the pasta is al dente.

Meanwhile bring a separate large saucepan of lightly salted water to the boil. Add the greens and cook briefly just to blanch. Drain and set aside.

Add the blanched greens and beans to the sausage mixture and stir well. Simmer, uncovered, for a further 5 minutes. Taste and adjust the seasoning. Stir in the basil and serve sprinkled with finely grated cheese and plenty of crusty bread on the side, if liked.

SERVES 4–6

112

This recipe makes a tasty meal out of the simplest ingredients. Bacon and leeks work well but feel free to add any other vegetables you have to hand.

MASHED POTATO PIE
with bacon, leeks & cheese

1 kg/2¼ lbs. floury potatoes, quartered

2 tablespoons olive oil

1 onion, finely chopped

2 small leeks, thinly sliced

80 g/3 oz. bacon, diced

30 g/2 tablespoons butter

250 ml/1 cup milk or single/light cream

1 egg, beaten

a large handful of fresh flat-leaf parsley leaves, chopped

a pinch of paprika

90 g/⅔ cup grated Cheddar

Put the potatoes in a large saucepan, add sufficient cold water to cover, salt well and bring to the boil. Simmer for about 20 minutes, until tender.

Meanwhile, heat the oil in a frying pan/skillet over low heat. Add the onion and leeks and cook gently for about 10 minutes, until soft. Add the bacon and cook for 3–5 minutes, until just browned. Season with salt and set aside.

Preheat the oven to 190ºC (375ºF) Gas 5.

Drain the potatoes and mash coarsely, mixing in the butter and milk. Season well and add the egg. Stir to combine.

Stir in the leek mixture, parsley, paprika and half the cheese. Transfer to a greased baking dish and spread evenly. Sprinkle over the remaining cheese and bake in the preheated oven for 35–45 minutes, until well browned. Serve immediately.

SERVES 4–6

115

There is nothing more homely than the
sweet smell of a delicious, freshly
made apple pie. Serve with cream.

classic
APPLE PIE

1 x 500-g/1 lb. 2-oz. pack sweet
shortcrust pastry, chilled

1.3 kg/3 lbs. apples, peeled, cored
and sliced

50 g/¼ cup sugar, plus extra for
sprinkling

1 teaspoon ground cinnamon

1 tablespoon freshly squeezed
lemon juice

1 egg, beaten, for brushing

cream, to serve

Using a rolling pin, roll out half the pastry on a lightly-
floured surface. Wrap the pastry loosely around the rolling
pin and then unwrap it over a greased pie dish, pressing it
into the bottom and sides. Trim the edges leaving a 1 cm/
½ inch overhang and save the pastry trimmings for
decoration if liked. Chill while you prepare the apples.

Put the apples in a bowl with the sugar, cinnamon and
lemon juice and use your hands to mix well. Transfer
to the pastry-lined pie dish.

Preheat the oven to 190°C (375°F) Gas 5.

Roll out the remaining pastry on a floured work surface to
a circle large enough to cover the apples. Brush the edges
of the pastry in the dish with beaten egg, then lay the
other pastry circle on top. Fold over the overhang from the
bottom layer and crimp using your fingertips, or use the
tines of a fork to seal. Decorate the top with a few leaves
cut out of the pastry trimmings, if liked, and brush lightly
with egg, then sprinkle with sugar. Cut 6–8 small slits in
the top of the pie.

Put the pie on a baking sheet and bake in the preheated
oven for about 50–60 minutes until golden. Serve warm
with chilled cream.

SERVES 6–8

just like mum used to make

With its sweet, fruity filling and sugary, crispy topping, this cobbler is the perfect dessert for a tea-time study break on a cold winter's day.

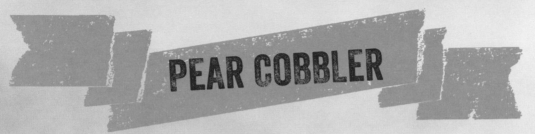

PEAR COBBLER

900 g/2 lbs. pears, peeled, cored and sliced

75 g/⅓ cup light brown sugar

2 tablespoons plain/all-purpose flour

1 teaspoon vanilla extract

finely grated zest of 1 orange

vanilla ice cream or whipped cream, to serve

Cobbler batter

300 g/3 cups plain/all-purpose flour

200 g/scant 1 cup sugar

1 tablespoon baking powder

a pinch of sea salt

250 ml/1 cup milk

115 g/1 stick butter, melted

extra sugar or cinnamon sugar, to sprinkle

Preheat the oven to 190°C (375°F) Gas 5.

In a bowl, combine the pears, sugar, flour, vanilla extract and orange zest. Toss gently with your hands to combine and arrange in an even layer in the bottom of a greased baking dish. Set aside.

To prepare the cobbler batter, combine the flour, sugar, baking powder and salt in a separate bowl. In a third bowl, stir together the milk and melted butter. Gradually pour the milk mixture into the dry ingredients, beating with a wooden spoon until just smooth.

Drop spoonfuls of the batter on top of the pears, leaving gaps but spreading to the edges. Sprinkle the top with sugar and bake in the preheated oven for about 40–50 minutes until golden brown. Serve warm with vanilla ice cream or whipped cream.

SERVES 4–6

just like mum used to make

This wicked popcorn is perfect for a movie night at home. Try adding some grated cheese while the popcorn is hot so it melts over the top.

paprika smoky bacon
POPCORN

50 g/½ cup crispy smoked bacon pieces/real bacon bits

1–2 tablespoons sunflower or vegetable oil

90 g/⅓ cup popcorn kernels

60 g/5 tablespoons butter

2 teaspoons smoked paprika

freshly ground black pepper

50 g/⅓ cup grated Cheddar, to serve (optional)

In a food processor, blitz the crispy smoked bacon pieces/real bacon bits to a fine powder and set aside.

Heat the oil in a large lidded saucepan with a few popcorn kernels in the pan. When you hear the kernels pop, carefully tip in the rest of the kernels. Shake the pan over the heat until the popping stops. Take care when lifting the lid as any unpopped kernels may still pop from the heat of the pan. Tip the popcorn into a bowl, removing any unpopped kernels as you go.

Melt the butter in a small saucepan over medium heat and then pour over the warm popcorn. Sprinkle over the bacon powder and paprika and stir well so the popcorn is evenly coated. Season to taste with black pepper. Add the cheese, if using, while the popcorn is still warm so that it melts onto the popcorn. Serve warm or cold.

MAKES
1 LARGE BOWL

PARTY ON DUDE!

PARTY ON DUDE!

These sticky sausages are so simple to prepare, you can whip up a quick batch without missing out on any of the fun at your party!

sesame SAUSAGES

12 chipolata sausages

2 tablespoons honey

2 tablespoons sesame seeds

Preheat the oven to 200°C (400°F) Gas 6. Twist the sausages in the middle and then cut in half.

Scatter the sausages over a heavy-based roasting dish and cook for 15–20 minutes, turning once. Drain off any fat. Add the honey and cook for another 15 minutes, turning a couple of times until the sausages are sticky and golden all over.

Sprinkle the sesame seeds over the sausages and cook for a further 5 minutes. Serve immediately.

SERVES 4

Perfect for sharing, this spicy, Mexican-style dip makes a great party snack. Serve with crunchy corn chips.

spicy BEAN DIP

440 g/2¼ cups dried black beans

2 tablespoons olive oil

1 red onion, chopped

4 garlic cloves, chopped

1 red (bell) pepper, deseeded and diced

1 tablespoon ground cumin

2 teaspoons dried oregano

2 teaspoons chilli/chili powder

2 x 400-g/14 oz. cans chopped tomatoes

a handful of fresh coriander/cilantro leaves, chopped

sour cream, to serve

warmed corn chips, to serve

Put the dried beans in a saucepan with 2 litres/8 cups cold water. Bring to the boil, then reduce the heat to a low simmer and cook the beans, uncovered, for about 1½ hours, until just tender and not falling apart. Drain well and set aside.

Heat the oil in a large, heavy-based saucepan over medium heat. When the oil is hot, add the onion, garlic and red pepper and cook for 8–10 minutes, until softened. Stir in the cumin, oregano and chilli/chili powder and fry for 1 minute, until the spices are aromatic.

Increase the heat to high. Add the tomatoes, beans and 250 ml/1 cup cold water and bring to the boil. Reduce the heat to low, partially cover the pan and cook for 1½–2 hours, adding a little more water from time to time if the mixture is drying or catching on the bottom of the pan. Transfer to a serving bowl and serve with the sour cream and coriander/cilantro on top and corn chips for dipping.

SERVES 6–8

Why go out for fried chicken when it's so easy to make at home? Serve with spicy potato wedges and creamy coleslaw for a southern-style feast.

spiced FRIED CHICKEN

3 skinless chicken breasts

150 ml/⅔ cup buttermilk

100 g/¾ cup plain/all-purpose flour

1 generous teaspoon baking powder

1 teaspoon sea salt

⅛ teaspoon ground cayenne pepper

½ teaspoon smoked paprika

¼ teaspoon ground coriander

¼ teaspoon garlic powder

a pinch of ground allspice

½ teaspoon dried oregano

black pepper

sunflower oil, for frying

Cut each chicken breast into 5 or 6 strips. Put them in a ceramic dish and coat with the buttermilk. Cover with clingfilm/plastic wrap and chill for at least 2 hours.

Remove the chicken from the buttermilk and pat off any excess with kitchen paper/paper towels. Combine the flour, baking powder, salt, spices, oregano and some black pepper in a bowl. Toss the chicken pieces in the seasoned flour and set aside on parchment paper for 10 minutes.

Pour 3–4 tablespoons sunflower oil in a frying pan/skillet. Set over medium heat and add one-third of the chicken pieces. Cook until golden and crispy. Drain on kitchen paper/paper towels and repeat with the remaining 2 batches of chicken.

SERVES 4

Jalapeños have a juicy flesh that is delicious combined with cheese. They can be quite spicy so this recipe is not for the faint hearted!

JALAPEÑO POPPERS

20 Jalapeño chillies/chiles
140 g/1¼ cups grated mature/sharp Cheddar
50 g/⅓ cup plain/all-purpose flour
1 egg, beaten
sunflower oil, for deep frying

Slit the Jalapeños along one side and carefully remove the seeds. Stuff them generously with the grated Cheddar.

Put the flour in one shallow bowl and the beaten egg in another. Roll the Jalapeños in the flour, dip in the egg and then coat once more with flour, ensuring that they are completely covered.

Half-fill a large saucepan with oil. Heat the oil until a cube of bread dropped into it browns in less than 60 seconds.

Fry the Jalapeños in small batches for 6–7 minutes until golden. Remove with a slotted spoon and drain on kitchen paper/paper towels. Serve immediately.

MAKES 20

When you bake fruit in the oven, the key is to not overcook it otherwise it will get too soft. Serve with plain yogurt or vanilla ice cream.

roasted
SOFT FRUIT

4 peaches or nectarines, or 8 plums or apricots, halved and pitted

3 tablespoons light brown soft sugar

1 teaspoon vanilla extract

30 g/2 tablespoons butter

plain yogurt or vanilla ice cream, to serve

Put the fruit in an ovenproof dish with the cut side facing upwards. Spoon the sugar evenly over each fruit half, add the vanilla extract and dot with little pieces of the butter.

Using oven gloves, put the dish in the oven and bake for 15–20 minutes. Serve immediately with plain yogurt or vanilla ice cream.

SERVES 4

nom nom nom
TREATS

Peanut butter and jelly are a common sandwich filling, but this traditional pairing taste even better when combined with chocolate.

peanut butter & jelly BROWNIES

125 g/4 oz. dark/bittersweet chocolate, chopped

100 g/7 tablespoons butter, diced

175 g/¾ cup plus 1 tablespoon sugar

3 eggs

100 g/¾ cup plus 1 tablespoon plain/all-purpose flour

a pinch of salt

4 generous tablespoons raspberry jelly/jam

peanut butter swirl

75 g/⅓ cup cream cheese

1 egg, lightly beaten

1 teaspoon vanilla extract

100 g/½ cup sugar

150 g/⅔ cup peanut butter

Preheat the oven to 170°C (325°F) Gas 3.

Make the peanut butter swirl first. Tip all the ingredients into a bowl and beat until smooth. Set aside.

Put the chocolate and butter in a heatproof bowl set over a saucepan of barely simmering water. Stir until smooth and thoroughly combined. Leave to cool slightly.

In a separate bowl, whisk the sugar and eggs for 2–3 minutes until light and foamy. Add the melted chocolate mixture and stir until combined. Sift the flour and salt into the bowl and fold in until well incorporated.

Spoon two-thirds of the brownie mixture into a 20 x 30-cm/8 x 12-inch baking pan, greased and lined with parchment paper, and spread level. Dot one-third of the peanut butter mixture and all of the raspberry jam over the brownie. Spoon over the remaining brownie mixture, then the remaining peanut mixture in equal spoonfuls. Using a round-bladed knife, swirl the mixtures together to create a marbled effect. Tap the pan on the work surface to level the mixture and bake on the middle shelf of the preheated oven for about 20–25 minutes.

Remove from the oven and leave to cool completely in the pan before removing and cutting into portions to serve.

MAKES 16–20

Perfect with a hot cup of tea, this spiced apple cake is just right for staving off hunger through those long afternoons in the library.

spiced apple
CAKE

225 g/2 sticks butter

200 g/1 cup light brown soft sugar

6 tablespoons honey

275 g/2 cups wholemeal/ wholewheat flour

75 g/⅔ cups plain/all purpose flour

2 teaspoons baking powder

1 teaspoon cinnamon

½ teaspoon each ground cloves, ginger and nutmeg

5 eggs, beaten

3 tablespoons ground almonds

50 g/½ cup sultanas/golden raisins

550 g/1 lb. 4 oz. any cooking apples, peeled, cored and finely chopped

4 tablespoons milk

3–4 tablespoons flaked almonds, toasted

icing/confectioners' sugar, for dusting

MAKES 16

Preheat the oven to 170ºC (325ºF) Gas 3.

Put the butter and brown sugar in a mixing bowl and cream together until light and fluffy. Beat in the honey. In a separate bowl, combine the flours, baking powder, cinnamon, cloves, ginger and nutmeg.

Fold the dry ingredients into the butter mixture, then add the eggs and mix well using a hand-held electric whisk. Fold in the ground almonds, sultanas/golden raisins, apples and milk and mix just to combine. Transfer the mixture to a greased 23 cm/9 inch square baking pan and level the top.

Bake in the preheated oven for about 50–60 minutes until risen and golden and a skewer inserted in the centre of the cake comes out clean. Let cool slightly in the pan then turn out onto a wire rack. When cool, sprinkle with flaked almonds and dust with icing/confectioners' sugar. Cut into squares to serve. The cake will keep in an airtight container for 4–5 days.

Sometimes you just need a little bite of something sweet. These sticky puddings are light and fluffy on top, with a pool of lemon sauce at the bottom.

magic citrus
PUDDINGS

freshly grated zest and freshly squeezed juice of 1 lemon

freshly grated zest and freshly squeezed juice of 1 lime

100 g/scant 1 cup sugar

50 g/4 tablespoons butter, softened

2 eggs, separated

75 g self-raising/self rising flour

250 ml/1 cup milk

Preheat the oven on to 180°C (350°F) Gas 4.

Put the lemon and lime zest in a mixing bowl. Add the sugar and butter and mix well until pale and fluffy. Add the egg yolks to the butter mixture in the mixing bowl and mix to combine. Stir in the lemon and lime juice. Add the milk and whisk to combine.

Whisk the egg whites in a separate, clean bowl until they are thick, white and form slight peaks.

Using a metal spoon, fold the egg whites into the mixture in the mixing bowl until just combined

Put 4–5 small, greased pudding basins in a deep baking dish. Spoon the pudding mixture into the basins and then pour water into the baking dish to come halfway up the sides of the basins. Bake in the preheated oven for 35 minutes, or until the puddings are light golden and cooked with a small pool of sauce in the bottom.

SERVES 4–5

Chocolate crispy cakes are quick and easy to prepare. Top them with popping candy for a super-fun popping effect.

popping popcorn
CRISPY CAKES

1–2 tablespoons sunflower or vegetable oil

50 g/3 tablespoons popcorn kernels

50 g/3½ tablespoons butter

125 ml/½ cup golden syrup/light corn syrup

150 g/5 oz. milk chocolate, broken into chunks

50 g/1 cup cornflakes

popping candy/space dust

coloured sprinkles or chocolate curls, to decorate

Heat the oil in a large lidded saucepan with a few popcorn kernels in the pan. When you hear the kernels pop, carefully tip in the rest of the kernels. Shake the pan over the heat until the popping stops. Take care when lifting the lid as any unpopped kernels may pop from the heat of the pan. Tip the popcorn into a mixing bowl, removing any unpopped kernels as you go.

Put the butter and syrup in a small saucepan and heat gently until the butter has melted. Add the chocolate and continue to heat, stirring constantly, until it has melted and you have a thick glossy sauce.

Add the cornflakes to the mixing bowl with the popcorn and pour over the chocolate sauce. Stir well to coat evenly.

Spoon the mixture into cupcake cases. Sprinkle each cake with a little popping candy and decorate with sprinkles or chocolate curls. Leave to set before serving.

MAKES 14

Enjoy these fruity muffins as a nutritious bite on the run or a mid-morning snack. They are even better spread with butter or cream cheese.

apple & raisin
MUFFINS

60 g/⅓ cup plain/
all-purpose flour

160 g/1 cup wholemeal/
wholewheat flour

110 g/½ cup dark brown soft
sugar

1 teaspoon bicarbonate
of soda/baking soda

½ teaspoon baking powder

1 teaspoon ground cinnamon

½ teaspoon ground allspice

a pinch of sea salt

250 ml/1 cup plain yogurt or milk

3 tablespoons vegetable oil

1 egg

4 tablespoons honey

100 g/⅔ cup raisins

1 small apple, cored and grated

1 teaspoon vanilla extract

Preheat the oven to 200°C (400°F) Gas 6.

Put the plain/all-purpose flour, wholemeal/wholewheat flour, sugar, bicarbonate of soda/baking soda, baking powder, cinnamon, allspice and salt in a large mixing bowl and stir to combine.

Mix the yogurt, oil, egg and honey in a separate mixing bowl and beat until well blended. Stir in half the raisins, apple and vanilla extract.

Pour the yogurt mixture into the flour mixture and mix to combine. Divide between paper cases lining a 9 or 12 hole muffin pan, filling them almost to the top. Sprinkle the remaining raisins on top of each muffin. Bake in the preheated oven for 25–35 minutes, until puffed and just brown around the edges. Let cool before serving. These muffins will keep for 2–3 days in an airtight container.

MAKES 9–12 ◣

141
nom nom nom treats

INDEX

RECIPE CREDITS

Laura Washburn
apple & raisin muffins
barley risotto with carrots
bean & cheese burritos
chicken meatballs with
    roasted onions & tomatoes
chipotle chicken & rajas tacos
classic apple pie
fish pie with leeks & herbs
ham & egg brunch quesadillas
honey & banana porridge
mashed potato pie with bacon,
    leeks & cheese
mixed vegetable tacos
moussaka
pear cobbler
pepper beef quesadillas
pizza soup
ravioli bake with grilled sweet
    peppers
sausage, pasta & bean stew
    with greens
shredded chicken tacos
spiced apple cake
steak, leek & mushroom pie
    with Guiness
tuna noodle casserole
vegetable pie

Annie Rigg
carrot & chickpea pancakes
chargrilled halloumi with
    mixed olive & herb tapenade
creamy bacon & onion tart
herby falafel with hummus &
    toasted flatbreads
peanut butter & jelly brownies
pizzette with assorted
    toppings
roasted vegetable salad with
    herby goat cheese
spiced fried chicken

Tonia George
baked tomatoes stuffed with
    goat cheese & herbs
blueberry pancakes
chickpea, tomato & chorizo
    soup
cous cous with feta, dill and
    spring greens
huevos rancheros
nutty honey granola

Amanda Grant
ham & pineapple pizzas
herby scrambled eggs
magic citrus puddings
roasted soft fruit
sesame sausages

Dan May
baked goat-cheese stuffed
    chicken breast
Cajun spiced baked potatoes
fruity quinoa & bean stew
jalapeno poppers
puttanesca pasta sauce
ultimate arrabiata pasta sauce

Ghillie Basan
chicken tandoori skewers
fiery beef skewers with satay
    sauce
peri peri shrimp skewers
roasted pumpkin wedges with
    lime & spices
spicy tofu skewers with soy
    dipping sauce

Sunil Vijayakar
beef & pea curry
butter chicken
chickpea masala
saag paneer
spinach dal
tarka dal

Fiona Smith
Greek barley salad
tuna & cannellini bean salad

Hannah Miles
paprika smoky bacon popcorn
popping popcorn crispy cakes

Miranda Ballard
big breakfast burger with a
    portobello mushroom & a
    fried egg

Susannah Blake
mushrooms on toast

Ross Dobson
spicy bean dip

PHOTOGRAPHY CREDITS

Steve Baxter
pages 59, 71, 72, 76, 94, 104,
126

Susan Bell
pages 23, 56, 131

Martin Brigdale
pages 55, 100, 103, 107, 109,
110, 113, 114

Peter Cassidy
pages 3, 4, 14, 21, 26, 29,
30, 31, 34, 37, 38, 42, 45, 46,
49–54, 58, 67, 73, 74, 80, 84,
91, 92, 98, 99, 101, 102, 105,
111, 112, 115, 117, 118, 120,
127, 128, 129, 130, 133, 135,
137, 141

Laura Edwards
pages 22, 81, 85, 123, 132

Tara Fisher
pages 86, 121, 122, 125, 134,
138, 139

Jonathan Gregson
pages 5, 15, 19, 20, 27

Richard Jung
pages 87, 89, 90, 93, 97

William Lingwood
pages 28, 57, 70, 82, 88, 95, 96

Steve Painter
pages 106, 108

William Reavell
pages 35, 36, 136

Kate Whitaker
pages 6, 7, 16, 17, 18, 32, 33,
60–61, 62, 63–66, 68, 69, 75,
77, 78, 83, 116, 119, 124, 140

Isobel Wield
pages 1, 2, 13, 25, 39, 40, 41,
43, 44, 47, 48

Clare Winfield
page 24